Crossing the Boundary

A Return to the Wilderness and Freedom

Also by Harriet Greene

Pampoody & Max
The Last Garage Sale
Within The Earth A Mountain
Jackson Whole Food Cookbook
Black Market Baby
Sculpting For Peace

Harriet Greene

Crossing the Boundary

A Return to the Wilderness and Freedom

Backroads Publishing

Published by Backroads Publishing
         9647 Wagner Creek Road
         Talent, Oregon 97540
         backroadspr@gmail.com

Printed in the United States of America

ISBN: 0-933294-10-7

Cover Illustration: Traversing Paintbrush Divide, Grand Teton
         National Park
         ©Watercolor by Martin Goldman

For Roanne

The bond we share in the mountains goes beyond the bond
between mothers and daughters. It has to do with wilderness,
the weather, two women walking. It is here that we survive
the perils of pollution, the pitfalls of family ties, the
unprecedented passing of time.

vi

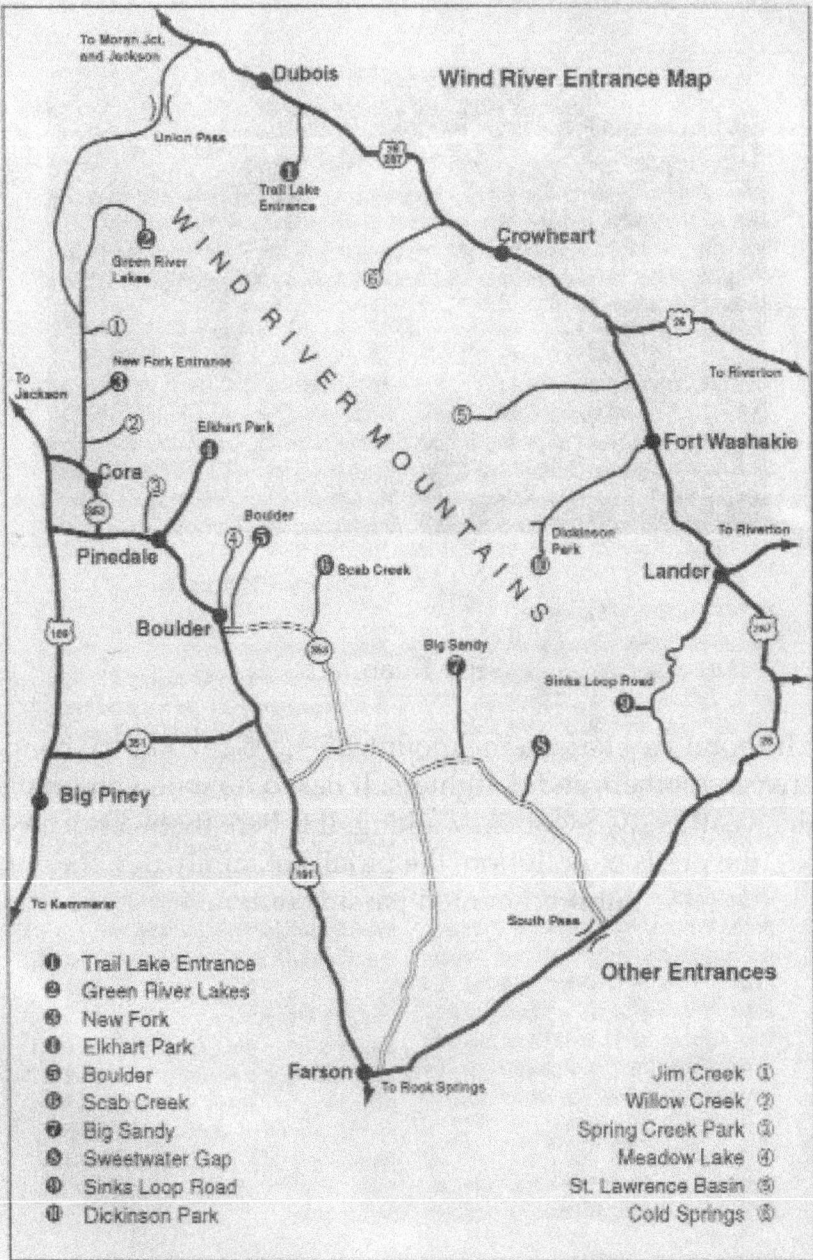

Wind River Entrance Map

Contents

Grand Teton National Park

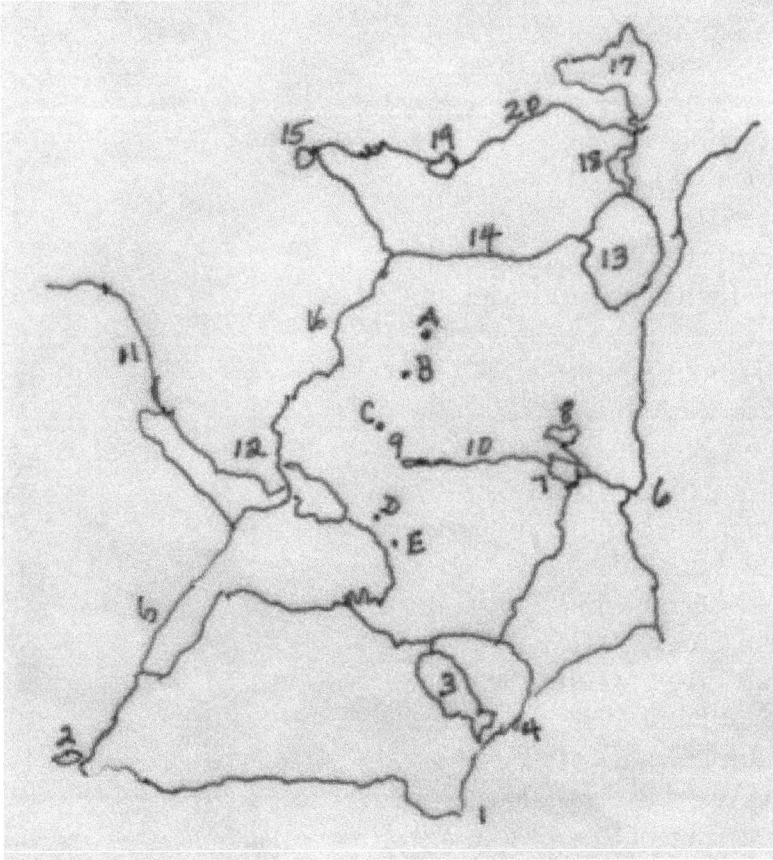

1. Granite Canyon Trailhead
2. Marion Lake
3. Phelps Lake
4. Death Canyon Trailhead
5. Teton Crest Trail
6. Taggart/Bradley Lakes
7. Taggart Lake
8. Bradley lake
9. Lake Taminah
10. Avalanche Canyon
11. Teton Canyon
12. Alaska Basin
13. Jenny Lake
14. Cascade Canyon
15. Lake Solitude
16. Hurricane Pass
17. Leigh Lake
18. String Lake
19. Holly lake
20. Paintbrush Canyon
A. Grand Teton
B. Middle Teton
C. South Teton
D. Buck Mountain
E. Static Peak

List of Illustrations

1. Avalanche Canyon, Snowdrift Lake, stonecut print
2. The Grand Tetons, stonecut print
3. Indian Paintbrush Divide, watercolor, Martin Goldman
4. Wildflowers, stonecut prints
5. Beach at Island Lake, Wind Rivers, August 1987
6. Valentine Lake
7. Grave Lake
8. Grave Lake/Mt. Chauvenet, Roanne
9. Mt. Chauvenet/Grave Lake, Karen
10. Peaks of East Fork Valley
11. Midsummer Dome, Pyramid Lake
12. Tent at Summit Lake
13. Twin Falls, Yoho National Park, pen & ink, Martin Goldman
14. Europe Canyon overlooking Milky Lakes, Roanne
15. Ramparts, Tonquin Valley, Jasper National Park, Alberta
16. Ramparts, Amethyst Lake, Jasper National Park, Alberta
17. Mushroom, Jasper National Park
18. Baldy Lakes, Wind Rivers, August 2000
19. Bald Mountain Basin, Angel Pass, 2000
20. Trees outside our tent, Bald Mountain Basin, 2000
21. Fire pit, Bald Mountain Basin, 2000
22. Campsite at Cook Lakes, 2000
23. Upper Cook Lake
24. Arnica, lower Cook Lake
25. Arnica, lower Cook Lake
26. Roanne's socks, North Fork Lake, August 2002
27. Mt. Victor, Europe Peak, 2002
28. Mt. Victor, from Victor Lake, 2002
29. Carson and Daniel at Prospector Lake, 2005
30. Black Joe Lake, 2005

x

Marble stonecut prints, sketches and photographs by the author unless otherwise stated. Since I am self-publishing I cannot afford to include color reproductions of my stonecut prints (most are in black and white) and photographs (color). If anybody wishes to see any of the work in color please email me and I will send a color copy of the piece/pieces.

Preface

Ever since I was eight years old I have been drawn to the outdoors. It all started in the Laurentian Mountains of southern Quebec where I spent summers at Camp Hiawatha. At fifteen, I returned as a senior and it was then that I was introduced to the wilderness.

Being too young in the earlier years to go on overnight expeditions, I remember enviously watching the older girls leave on canoe trips. I wanted so much to do this but we had to "swim the lake," just over a quarter of a mile, and pass a critical canoe test before our names could be added to the list of candidates. My counselor, who was head of the waterfront, helped me through these tests, and one morning twenty of us sang our way out of camp as the truck pulling six canoes headed north for five days in the Quebec wilderness. We paddled until we couldn't feel our arms, ate mostly canned peaches because one of the supply canoes had tipped while rushing to cross a lake one stormy afternoon, slept in a long tent made up of a tarp stretched between two distant trees and pegged along each side, and arrived back at camp, heroic, drenched and dirty but very happy. I couldn't wait to do it again.

As an only child and adopted, I had had a sheltered upbringing. My parents watched me like a hawk. But in the great outdoors I could forget who I was and where I came from. There were trees, infinite sky, mountains and lakes; a summer storm with nowhere to hide; eating outside with no table manners; being dirty without reprimand; away from all that was familiar and taking risks rather than remaining in reassured comfort. It was all about freedom.

When I married and had kids I moved to the suburbs. Canasta didn't work for me; neither did golf nor hanging out at playgrounds and shopping centers. In 1969 we moved to Vermont, just across the border from Montreal, where I could walk in the woods, while away hours at the waterfall, breathe easier and generally feel unfettered.

After a bitter divorce, my partner, Marty, and I, along with my three daughters – Karen, Maxine, and Roanne – moved to Wyoming and settled into a small log cabin in the tiny town of Wilson at the foot of the Grand Tetons. However, Roanne, my youngest, and I were left to continue our wilderness adventures alone when my two older girls decided to return to Vermont and remain with their father, visiting during the summer months – sometimes.

Each of my daughters is special in her own way, but the one thing we share is our love for the mountains. We have all walked together since they could stand. Starting in Stowe, Vermont, areas of the Long Trail (America's first long-distance hiking trail) around Mt. Mansfield in the Green Mountains, and Mt. Washington in New Hampshire's White Mountains demanded a few trips. I remember carrying one of my daughter's skis and boots along with mine up the icy, rutted, five-mile road, the last few in the dark for a ski down Hillman's Highway.

I began writing about my backpacking trips while living in the West. This was a new experience – the Rockies – hiking above timberline, in fields of wildflowers, boulders as big as buildings, amongst wildlife – moose, bear, elk. I was mesmerized with these mountains.

A number of these trips have been included in two previous books (hikes 1 through 6 appear in *Within the Earth a Mountain*; hikes 7 through 15 appear in *Black Market Baby*) because I had never planned on writing a book entirely about my backpacking trips until now. I am seventy-six years old at this writing, and have a lot of miles behind me. I love being in the wilderness. That is what has defined my life. I left the city for the country and never went back.

Crossing the boundary means crossing from National Forest into Wilderness where one is on her own. It also means crossing from the physical boundary of the body into the emotional boundary of the mind; facing your relationship with your child and her relationship with her mother. And what do you learn in all that time on all those trips? Independence, survival and how to relate to the closest person in the world to you – a daughter to her mother, a mother to her daughter.

After the divorce that shattered our storybook existence, and we didn't know it then, but it would be walking in the wilderness where we were able to find the time to free the frozen feelings and piece our lives back together again.

In crossing boundaries you leave one set of rules for another. If you're not ready to make a change in your life, you are not prepared to cross any boundary – whether it be physical, emotional or spiritual. You have to know how to pack your gear properly, be prepared to be honest with yourself, be willing to accept the pain.

I chose this title because of the freedom and joy I feel crossing the wilderness boundary at the beginning of our hikes and how at the end I turn back repeatedly to stare at the sign that finally vanishes in the distance and reluctantly continue, knowing I have to wait until our next adventure to feel the crossing.

Acknowledgments

Special thanks to:

-- my daughter Roanne, my friend and partner, who pushed for every trip into the mountains; who shouldered most of the weight as I got older; who put up with my anxiety over weather and bears and constantly having to check with rangers as to their latest reports; who understood my apprehension of dealing with sheer drop-offs; who did most of the cooking when I was exhausted after a long day of hiking. She put up with a great deal and in exchange I left her with the legacy of my love for the wilderness.
-- my husband Marty, who understood my love of backpacking, my need to get into the mountains with my daughter, and never complained of my mountain sojourns; also my editor who has the ability to see the whole picture from his years as a filmmaker/director – the characters, setting, props, rhythm and sound of the scenes/chapters. However I am my final editor, for better or worse . . .
-- my dear friend and grammar/punctuation editor, Bonnie Brown Koeln, who knows I couldn't get along without her.
-- Cheryl Koski who gave me permission to include her husband's letter in my book.

Grateful acknowledgment is made to the following publishers, authors and agencies for permission to reprint material copyrighted or controlled by them:

Sky's Witness, A Year in the Wind River Range by C.L. Rawlins, Pg. 87-88, Henry Holt and Co. Inc., 115 West 18th St., NY 10011
The Wilderness in Our Genes by George Duffy, New Mexico Wilderness Alliance newsletter.
Pilgrimage Santiago, Derek W. Youngs
The Selected Journals of Henry David Thoreau

Peace Pilgrim, Her Life and Work in Her Own Words. Ocean Tree
       Books, Box 1295, Santa Fe, N.M. 87504
Leave No Trace, Center for Outdoor Ethics
Wind River Trails by Finis Mitchell
Wilderness sign photo: USFS photo
Quote by John Muir in a letter to his sister Rachel, 1873
Wind River Entrance Map, courtesy of Rebecca Woods
"Wilderness": "Credit: Wilderness Watch."
"There is a tide...." Quote by William Shakespeare from Julius
       Caesar

Introduction

Walking in the mountains is a unique experience. One becomes an integral part of nature. You see and hear things that you couldn't notice traveling by bike or car or, least of all, by plane. Our bodies are made to walk. It improves circulation, increases lung capacity, massages meridians stimulating our nervous system, and promotes a general feeling of well-being. It doesn't cost anything. It gives us time to think and to dream – both left and right brain experiences. Walking is wonderful and in a world of turmoil it offers peace and quiet.

At the end of the day, after a long hike, my body tingling and mind calm, I feel as if I've been away. I become sensitive to the ebb and flow of life, the crystalline images created by clear air, and conscious of a three-dimensional feeling of space around me. Any troubles, problems or doubts either seem more remote or have been resolved.

This book is a compilation of backpacking trips that my daughter Roanne and I (the first three trips included my two older daughters as well) have taken over a period of twenty-six years from 1979 to 2005 after our move from Stowe, Vermont to Jackson Hole, Wyoming where we spent years hiking in Grand Teton National Park and the Wind Rivers; a move to the Canadian West opened us up to Banff, Jasper and Yoho National Parks in the Rockies, and the Kokanee Glacier Provincial Park in Nelson, British Columbia; the Taos Mountains on the west lobe of the Sangre de Cristos beckoned after relocating to northern New Mexico. Our trips lasted from a few days to a few weeks and over the years we learned how to survive in the mountains and respect their wildness. We also came to the realization that wilderness was essential to our relationship and our lives.

Why do I walk? Beauty. You have to walk enough with a load so that the weight becomes secondary and loses its demand on you physically; so you can enjoy the beauty around you. The world is such a beautiful place. But beauty is not beauty without its opposite: the ugliness of cramped quarters, of narrow minds,

2

of poverty and need, of greed and hatred, of racism . . .

and then there is the wilderness.

The List

The list is the most important document, more so than my birth certificate, driver's license and deed to my house. Without a list, there is no way I would venture into the mountains for more than a day! And even with a list we once forgot toilet paper; and another time, my watch so that I could watch the hours pass through the night and know how long until first light; and once we couldn't find our matches (we had them for the first two days but then a bear stopped by and needed a match) . . . but were lucky enough to beg some off another hiker because he was leaving. So there is nothing more essential than "The List."

FOOD

Breakfast (per day): 1-1¼ c. barley/oat flakes, 2 T. flaxseed, stevia, dried fruit, nuts
Lunch (per day): bagels (½/person/lunch), bread slices, rice cakes/corn crackers, nori sheets, jam, tahini, almond/peanut butter, carrot sticks, avocado (if ambitious)
Dinner (per day): couscous (½ c.) or pasta + freeze-dried vegetables (1½ c.); freeze-dried rice and beans (½ c.), dried tofu, shitake mushrooms (2/day every other day)
Snacks: fruit leather, dried fruit, seeds, nuts, miso candy (1-2/day), bars, hummus powder, broth powder, miso, chili powder , kuzu, salt, tea bags

UTENSILS/EQUIPMENT
stove, paper clip for stove shield, fuel
tent, material repair kit, extra string, ground sheet
sleeping bag
foam pads
dog bowl, food
rope to hang food
cooking pots, spoons, forks, mugs

water filter/purifier
1 gallon plastic folding container for water storage
food storage sacks

CLOTHING
tights
boots, flip-flops/sandals
handkerchief
bandanna (neck sun protection)
wool hat and gloves
hat (sun protection)
down vest and jacket, rain parka
sweater (wool)
shirt (light blouse), long sleeve for sun protection
duofolds (double layer long underwear, top and bottom)
t-shirts – one short and one long sleeve
shorts and long pants (quick-drying good idea)
socks – 2 - 3 pairs

MISCELLANEOUS
camera, film/binoculars
pad and pencils, plastic tube for pencils
book
sewing kit, extra shoelaces
hip pack (day hikes)
Swiss army knife (other)
flashlight, spare batteries/bulb, solar charger
floss, toothbrush, brush/comb, towel
first aid kit
unscented lotion, insect repellent, sunscreen, lip balm
watch
matches (waterproof container), lighter
toilet paper/plastic trowel
maps/compass
water bottle and carrier
candles
sunglasses

I

First Teton Trip

August 1979:

It had been a little over a year since I had seen my two older daughters. After the divorce, they had decided to stay with their father in Vermont rather than come west with Roanne, Marty and me. I had asked them to visit this summer and waited hopefully for a positive reply. It came. I booked airline tickets and, a week later, Roanne and I drove to Idaho Falls to pick them up.

My heart skipped a beat as they suddenly materialized out of the approaching crowd. They looked older, apprehensive, and our hugs were hesitant. We didn't talk much on the way home or while our backpacks were filled for three days of hiking in the Grand Tetons. Awkward and estranged.

Karen, Roanne, Me and Maxine

Marty dropped us off at the Death Canyon trailhead and waved good-bye as if he'd never see us again. Roanne was eleven, Maxine, fourteen, Karen, sixteen, and I, thirty-eight. Under a blue, cloudless sky the four of us walked along the trail now overgrown with elephanthead, cow parsnip and monkshood, all five feet high and more, monkeyflowers, sticky geraniums, Indian paintbrush, lupine and harebells. On the first switchback down to Phelps Lake I passed the spot where, earlier in the season, I had seen two leopard lilies (fritillaries).

After the cutoff to the lake we made our way through a forest of large cottonwoods, huge Engelmann spruce and jungle-like undergrowth and started to climb the steep switchbacks between the massive walls of Death Canyon; rocks that have been folded, faulted and fractured, their faces stained by numerous silvery run-offs.

Roanne tired quickly, complaining about her pack that was almost the same size as she was. I took it and balanced it on top of mine. This was going to be a difficult trip. Karen and Maxine took turns carrying it as well until the top that seemed to take forever. The canyon had finally broadened and leveled out to become a beautiful panorama of greens and endless wildflowers.

Lunch beside a waterfall. Billowy, white, cotton clouds provided some shade and a cool breeze.

Maxine developed blisters on the backs of her heels and we stopped to rest and soak our feet in one of the jade-colored pools formed by the meandering stream.

To the west, the Death Canyon shelf was visible with Mt. Bannon, Mt. Jedediah Smith and Mt. Meek rising behind it. Horses grazing in the trees surprised us as did the pack trip that owned them. Waterfalls and rushing streams cascaded down the forested sides of the canyon. How many lakes were up there? How pretty they must be.

Somewhere in-between the two camping zones Roanne discovered that her favorite green John Deere hat that had been with her forever was missing. Somebody who passed us later on said that he had seen it and left it on a rock. She was bummed. So was I but too tired to go back.

The camping zone appeared at the head of the canyon, about seven and a half miles in, at the end of a long, tiring, hot, exasperating day and a campsite was eventually found in a stand of evergreens beside the creek. Our ancient, orange tent went up on ground layered with sweet-smelling pine needles. I don't remember exactly what dinner was but all of us were so exhausted, it didn't matter.

Squashed into the tent, the three of us lay lengthwise and Roanne across the head – she was still small enough then. We talked until the shells of the sunflower seeds grew into a mound. I don't know when I fell asleep but sometime in the middle of the night Maxine frightened us when she thought she heard a bear prowling around the tent.

"Ma, did you hear that?"

"What?" I whispered back.

"Listen, there's a bear out there. There it is again."

I listened hard. Between the wind, the gurgling of the nearby creek and everybody's breathing I couldn't hear anything. What was that? Oh God! There was something out there – a rustling in the leaves!

What the hell was I going to do with three kids in a tent in the middle of the night and a wild animal outside! Was I crazy bringing my daughters into the mountains alone with nothing to insure our safety? I did hear something out of the ordinary but, if it were a bear, wouldn't it make more noise? There was other wildlife like deer, elk, moose, marmots, squirrels . . .

Where were those damn sunflower hulls? Maybe it was the smell that attracted him. Well, I couldn't do anything about that now.

"I'm going out to see," Maxine uttered.

"No you're not." I commanded. "Don't move. Just sit tight and maybe it'll go away . . . if it's there at all."

"Just go to sleep, Maxine, and stop getting us all crazy," Karen whispered. Roanne didn't wake up at all.

What should I do? Nothing. Maxine finally fell asleep and I stood watch for the rest of the night. I might have dozed on and off because shadows finally appeared where there were none before, a preface of dawn.

Day 2: Cold and clear. The sun's first rays turned the rocks on top of the shelf to gold and gradually crept down the canyon walls until its warmth reached us.

Roanne had made a momentous decision. Embarrassed by what had happened the day before, she confessed to all of us that, from now on, she was going to shoulder her own load and not let anybody carry her pack ever again. She never has. I guess she realized how much fun it was to be where we were and do what we were doing. Whatever the reason, she actually got involved with what you had to do to get into the mountains. It gave her the independence she loves and the freedom to travel wherever she wants. She became a hiker.

Breakfast is an anticipated event in the mountains. Our dispositions had improved from yesterday. With spirits high and bellies full, we headed up to Fox Creek Pass through fields of lupine, daisies and showy fleabane. The trail was steep and frequent stops were made to rest and cool off, accomplished by wetting our bandanas and squeezing them over our heads. A large, perpetual snowfield provided us with pleasure as we tossed snowballs at each other and into the air. Finding snow in July is pure joy.

An old trapper's cabin sent our imaginations spinning into the "once upon a time" land of old western movies like "Shane." Who had lived here? I wished I had.

Back to reality and 5.7 miles to Alaska Basin. Roanne mumbled a made-up mantra that got her across the shelf and up Mt. Meek Pass. Descending Sheep's Steps, switchbacks leading over the limestone wall with bits of snow still clinging to the ledges blocking the trail, the four of us finally entered the basin; wall-to-wall wildflowers, glaciated rock, sparkling streams and waterfalls, lakes and trails in every direction. At Sunset Lake, fringed with flowers, the tent went up on uneven ground beside a clump of trees.

Fox Creek Pass

Roanne, Maxine and Karen on the Death Canyon Shelf

Sunset Lake

Roanne, a bandaid on her little toe and her pail beside her, cut a very cute picture standing on a tuft of grass in the water by the shore, washing her hair – no soap – while dinner cooked. It was awful – some kind of packaged camper's stew. The lake suddenly dropped into shade while the peak of the Grand, the only part of it we could see through a dip in the Avalanche Wall, glowed orange in the setting sun. The day had been optimistic and exhilarating. All of us felt good, although exhausted, but ready for Hurricane Pass the next morning.

Day 3: It was a long thirteen miles out – the climb to Hurricane Pass and then mostly downhill – which played havoc on our knees and hips. A pack trip with horses carrying gear and riders climbed the switchbacks, passed us and in no time, reached the top. Not a bad way to travel.

Lots of tiny pools at the head of the south fork; wet and boggy; five miles to the forks. It was nice to stretch out along flat Cascade Canyon, so nice that we lingered too long and had to run to catch the boat across Jenny Lake in the last rays filtering through the mountain peaks. Dinner at Dornan's Chuckwagon ended a glorious day.

That first trip opened up a whole world behind the peaks where only our footsteps could take us and launched endless treks into the Tetons for the next ten years. There was never any question where to go but which loop to make. This trip reinforced our passion for hiking in the wilderness together, renewed our family ties, and re-established our love for one another that sometimes wore thin during long absences.

12

II

The Lightning Storm

August 1984:

Karen arrived in her beige VW bug from Vancouver, British Columbia, and Maxine, off a plane from Halifax, Nova Scotia. It was time for a walk in the wilderness. Roanne, always smiling when her sisters were around, and Karen, worked on the food while Maxine cut plastic tarps for our ancient, orange tents. It had been five years since our last hike and the single orange tent had now become two. I watched, happy to have all of us back together again!

Packed up that night for an early start the next morning. Marty dropped us off on the Idaho side of the Teton Range at the trailhead to the south fork of Teton Canyon, one of the routes across the mountains. Alaska Basin, a wide valley scoured by successive glaciers and noted for its spectacular wildflower displays, was our goal.

Easy and flat. Three miles in, just past the junction to Devil's Stairs, the trail began to climb. Following the turbulent creek, we switchbacked up to a bench and finally had no choice but to cross it.

There was a large log with only a thin, flexible wire stretched from one side to the other that offered no support. It was just there. This was not for me or Maxine or Roanne. But Karen made the attempt, and, slowly, balancing her heavy pack while placing one foot precariously in front of the other, reached midway and, for a moment, I thought she might turn back – it was a long way across – she faltered, caught herself and continued on in deep concentration while I held my breath, not moving, not wanting to distract her. She finally stepped onto solid ground, looked back at us, smiled, and proudly took a few bows.

Now it was our turn. Throwing our boots across to her and plunging into the mid-thigh, icy water, clinging to one another, Maxine, from her Outward Bound experience, told us to unbuckle our belts, letting our backpacks hang loose. Just in case the current was too strong and swept us downstream, our packs were freed up and wouldn't weigh us down. Midway I felt the water tugging at me. Every time I moved a leg forward, it would be pulled downstream and I had to force it back and keep moving. It was freezing, the rocks were slippery and we clung to one another against the brutal force of the rushing water. Karen cheered us on until, one by one, she dragged us onto the bank. Our legs were numb, but our spirits were high, our bodies charged. Some of the tension was released after this challenge and we warmed up towards one another.

The second crisis was the realization that I had my camera, two lenses and no film. NO FILM! Need I say more.

The canyon widened and the four of us climbed the bedrock floor to another bench. From nowhere a young boy, about eight, appeared. He was spending the summer with his father who was a ranger. How lucky can one be to run around Alaska Basin day after day!

Up and onto another bench where Two Island Lake, one of the many small basin lakes, was nestled. It was late afternoon and I couldn't have gone much farther. The girls set up the tents while I sat on a warm, smooth rock, resting my aching muscles and stiff back – two tents, side by side, facing west and the setting sun. All of us played in the lake, got wet to our waists, then walked around to the rocks jutting into the water.

Maxine didn't care to join us but remained alone on a rock, doing I don't know what, just being contrary. Why does she do this? Too much competition? A cry for attention? Does she just like to be alone? Strained feelings. A ripple in the day. I felt that she wasn't happy. But I couldn't do anything about it. I don't know this child anymore. Why do I worry? I guess I still think she's a little girl and shouldn't be left alone by the water. Am I confused! Doesn't she know I love her and want her to be with me for the short time we have together? That's the mother in me.

The reality is that we are different now – so much time has passed, so much miscommunication. These are problems I don't want to deal with at the present. I want to be out and free and having a good time. And I want her to feel the same way. A mother's wish – only in my dreams.

Our two tents in Alaska Basin

Dinner was prepared while watching the sun go down in an orange sky mirrored in the glassy lake – no wind – and the four of us relaxed in the beauty of a peaceful evening.

Day 2: At six a.m. I went out to answer the call of nature and then sat on a rock. Pink clouds reflected in a calm, turquoise lake. Quiet and motionless amid mountain slopes blazing with rainbow colors of countless wildflowers. Paradise.

The girls stirred. I thought about my two older daughters and our life back east when we had all been together. There was always a lot of fighting, something I could never get used to,

having been an only child. The sibling rivalry was mainly
between Karen and Maxine. Roanne always seemed happy. How
does one go about raising a child, handling deep-seated
emotions made up of pieces of past lifetimes, the astrological
blueprint and the normal Freudian roles within the family unit?
We are such complex beings. All the people who claim to have
the answers seem to have the nuttiest kids.

Buck Mountain, a vast titanic temple, silhouetted on the
eastern skyline, was cloaked in mist. A gentle breeze riffled the
water, distorting its reflections of pink and soft blue. The lake
responded instantly to every subtle change of clouds, wind or
atmosphere. So do children.

Hurricane Pass

After breakfast and packing up for our climb to Sunset Lake
(having camped there five years ago) and Hurricane Pass, the
four of us moved slowly up the steep slope, wading knee-deep
in wildflowers until a switchback blocked by snow stopped me. I
faced the wall of snow, looked straight up to where I had to go,

back to the edge I was on, and didn't want to move. The girls backtracked to where I was stuck, kicked footsteps into the snow, hauled me up and continuing, puffed our way to the top.

Battleship Mountain, a massive rock, loomed to the west, the Teton Peaks to the east while traversing the ridge that divided Grand Teton National Park from Targhee National Forest, then picked our way down the snow-covered headwall of the south fork of Cascade Canyon. The crevasses of Schoolroom Glacier

Karen, Roanne and Maxine on the way to the Wall

and the bergshrund (the crevasse where the ice of the moving glacier had pulled away from the rock wall) came into view.

Dark clouds were forming while hiking around the tiny lake of glacial melt trying to meet up with the old Skyline Trail, abandoned many years ago because of unsafe rock at the base of the wall.

A few raindrops. The trail was difficult to find. Hail. Up over ten thousand feet and miles from nowhere. No shelter, nothing. Lightning. This was getting serious. We dropped our packs and ducked under a large rock, covering ourselves with the plastic used as rainflies for the tents.

Thunder cracked rattling our insides, and lightning bolts bounced off boulders around us, too close for comfort. I could actually see this happen. Karen panicked and started to tear away the covering. I grabbed her and held her close. "Don't move. Just sit tight." She was petrified. All of us were. There was nothing to do. We were in God's hands.

The hail hit the plastic hard. While trying desperately to shrink farther under the rock, I said a silent prayer that if my daughters and I survived, the four of us would become friends forever or make one heck of an attempt.

It seemed an eternity until the hail stopped and the rain subsided. The lightning flashed in the near distance and the thunder rumbled, echoing amidst the peaks. A bit of blue appeared and, emerging from our makeshift shelter doubtfully looking around, found it amazing to still be alive.

We donned our packs and backtracked down to the trail left about an hour ago, hiked to the forks near tree line and sat on a wet rock for some cheese and crackers. The sky was threatening. Lightning still flashed. There was a decision to be made – to walk out to a dry home or walk up to Avalanche Canyon and take a chance on the weather.

Sitting in silence, neither of us wanted to cut the trip short nor disappoint one another. "I'm not sure." "I don't know." "What do you think?" "It's hard to tell." This was a formidable decision. These high mountain storms can be dangerous.

Since all of us had an adventuresome spirit, a reluctant decision to try for the heights prevailed. With eyes to the sky, our ponchos within reach, some dried fruit in our pockets, we plunged ahead – a little over a mile and a half up to the Divide – and who knows where from there.

Sloshing through wet snow and mud, the trail disappeared and reappeared. The Wall, a remnant of ancient limestone beds that once topped the Teton Range, stretched out in front of us and, a moment later, the top at 10,600 feet was gained. Clouds were moving fast overhead as Kit and Snowdrift Lakes appeared far below. A steep, treacherous snowfield lay between the lakes and us. Ice axes would have been useful. The four of us looked at one another, scared, and knew it was vital to get off this high divide.

The girls down-climbed in the steep rocks while I sledded on my folded poncho with my backpack dragging behind, digging into the snow to slow me down, and slid undignified to the bottom. Not much flat ground, maybe enough for two tents. They were up in record time and we were in them just as the first drops fell. The rain beat down and high winds ballooned the sides of the tents. Warm and cozy inside, each of us wondered if the right decision had been made.

As suddenly as it had begun, the rain stopped and the sun came out. The sky was blue again, the wind subsided and clouds floated above. Our wet clothes were spread outside, our soggy boots kicked off while running around trying to avoid stepping on tiny alpine laurel and forget-me-nots; nothing like a near-death crisis to bring a family together.

I thought of Marty back home thinking about us. The storm had been unusually intense and I knew he would be worried.

Our clothes dried just in time. The sky darkened and the wind blew rain over the Wall and down on us. Talked until it got dark. Changing partners every night, Maxine and I crawled into one tent. She gave me her watch so I could see the hours go by and maybe sleep a little.

During the night frightening noises reverberated within the canyon walls, screeches that were unidentifiable. They were close to the tent, then changed direction until they faded only to continue again after short intervals. Hawks? Owls? They kept me awake while my exhausted kids slept like babies, unaware of

20

Avalanche Canyon Wall, Snowdrift Lake

a watchful mother's eye. It rained sporadically most of the night, that slow persistent rain that never seems to tire, and lightning lit up the tent like the middle of the afternoon.

I tried to sleep but when I opened my eyes it was so black, I couldn't define anything and panicked. Struggling desperately to see something, I unzipped the tent and fled into the night . . . realizing that I couldn't see anything out there either.

"What are you doing, Ma?" a sleepy voice murmured.

"I got claustrophobic, Maxine. It's so dark."

"Ma, come inside, it's pouring."

Groping for the tent, I staggered around on the wet grass. Following the direction of her voice, I suddenly stumbled back inside, tripping over the open flap. I stripped off my wet clothes and climbed into a warm sleeping bag.

"What I need is a new spacious tent."

That irrational fear of being confined was gone after a few deep breaths of night air and I settled down to listen to the beating of my heart. But I had to work hard at controlling that incessant need to get out and move around, the same way Karen had felt while waiting under our tarp for the storm to pass.

I watched Maxine sleep and remembered the hours I would spend with my middle child, desperately trying to communicate. She was stubborn, blocked to everything emotional. At other times a light would go on and we would get it together, whatever "it" was. Strange that she chose to stay behind after the divorce or maybe not so strange. Maybe that's her karma. And mine.

A number of years ago when she was spending the summer with me, we did cry together. She admitted not being sure she had made the right decision; neither was I to have left her. But that's how it turned out. One never knows.

Well, this storm helped out. It brought us together and showed us that all of us still cared deeply for one another. I watched the hours go by and waited for morning which finally dawned bright and clear.

Day 3: Everything was dry. After a breakfast of oatmeal, raisins, milk and peppermint tea, a walk along the north side of Snowdrift Lake with the South Teton and Nez Perce to the north, Mt. Wister and Veiled Peak to the south, the Wall to the west, brought us to the edge. Suddenly, Lake Taminah, narrow and long, came into view far below. Dropped off the bench and picked our way down the steep drainage – no trail; a vertical snowfield with the muffled sound of rushing water beneath. I didn't like it. Karen was in front. Maxine held one of my hands, and Roanne the other, and slowly, slipping and sliding, all of us finally reached firm ground.

Down to the lake – about a mile – and along its north shore – wet and rocky. The thunder of Shoshoko Falls could be heard as we approached the rim of the Taminah bench and inched our way across another precipitous snowfield; climbed down rock slabs and scrambled through gullies while hanging on to dry, scraggy branches and gnarled, exposed roots. A gymnastic descent.

Which way to go? No trail, no cairns, nothing; acres of boulders, steep and scary. Stuck on ground surrounded on three sides by rushing water, the climb back up left us exhausted. I had mapped out an imaginary trail while above treeline, laid it out very carefully but all was forgotten down below. I couldn't find any of my mental markers. It was difficult to see up ahead and plan a safe retreat. Bushwhacking to the bottom, I hoped to avoid getting hung up on a cliff.

The falls broke up into numerous streams that spread out around us; crossed and re-crossed creeks, not bothering to take off boots anymore, wondering which side of the canyon to be on. Ideal moose habitat. Animals had bedded down in the deep grass for the night – their imprints visible – and the thought of startling a large animal was unnerving. Hours went by and still no trail. I was becoming apprehensive.

Suddenly, on the north side of the canyon, a flash of red. I yelled. Two girls, the first human beings seen for days, were hiking back from the falls. Relieved and happy, the four of us splashed through knee-high water to the opposite bank and climbed to a real trail.

I have never before been so thrilled to walk in the middle of a well-worn path. But it didn't last. There were more boulder fields to cross and thick woods to penetrate, over and under fallen tree trunks. Down, we kept going down. As the hikers disappeared ahead, I ran after them, afraid of losing the elusive trail. I finally caught up and gave them two dimes to call Marty when they got back to work and tell him to meet us.

What was that blue shimmering in the distance? Could it be Taggart Lake? Had our intrepid little band covered four and a half miles since the falls?

Moose bogs. Wet, wet, wet. A lot of game trails taking off in every direction and the lake, finally at our feet. A long walk around it brought us to our favorite rock and totally spent, we climbed on it to rest and calm down.

Our boots and socks weren't worth putting on again. The cool, dry ground felt good under our waterlogged, spongy soles finally in flip-flops for the last mile and a half to civilization. An elderly gentleman in the parking lot was drinking something out of a can. He invited us to the back of his pickup and threw open a cooler that was filled with real ice cubes and cans of pop.

Our mouths watered. I offered to buy four cans but he told us to help ourselves and tell him where we had been. So, while waiting for Marty, hoping the girls had called him, our adventures were recounted while drinking refreshing, cold, delicious pop from a can.

Scratched from head to toe, muddy and wet, and happy to see our blue and white VW van tooling down the road. Hugs and kisses. Sheer delight. Yes, he had watched the storm and even went outside to experience what the four of us were going through in the mountains. He said it was one of the worst storms he had ever seen in the valley. So did the news on the radio. This had been a hike never to forget, a mark in our memories that would remain for our lifetimes. My daughters and I were closer then than we had been for years.

III

Teton Crest Trail

September 1986:

Roanne wrote: "I like having sisters." I know she does but hasn't lived with them since we left for Wyoming eight years ago. This was a blow to both of us, one that we have never been able to get over. She misses them as I do. The years pass and all of us grow further and further apart, losing the feeling of family. But we kept writing and calling. Summer vacations were walks in the wilderness where the four of us could spend a few days away from the pressures and patterns of civilized ties.

1985 had slipped by. This summer only Karen turned up. We met her at the airport and, after dropping Roanne off at her summer job's staff party, Karen and I went out for dinner alone, something neither of us had ever done – a Mexican beer for her, some Saki for me and a Chinese meal that kept us laughing and talking for hours. She told me about her life and I listened. She was living with a guy, going to art school and waitressing in the evenings. My oldest daughter was fun to be with.

Karen filled her backpack while I checked the list to make sure she had everything needed – an easy task we all had been doing for years. During the day Roanne and I had prepared the food, enough for five days, so when she came home from her party late that evening, the two of them disappeared into her teepee where they would spend the night.

Up early in the morning and ready to leave for the Teton Crest Trail, a route that traverses the length of the Teton Range along the hydrographic divide. Granite Canyon looked unfriendly at 8 a.m. and a short ways in Karen spotted a bear and her cub lumbering up the mountainside just ahead. They were moving in another direction and that was fine with us.

The Grand Tetons

Our packs were heavy and the going was tough. The trail wound through the woods, cool and fragrant, and gradually climbed, sometimes staying high above Granite Creek, sometimes winding through the willows alongside the water. Just after the ranger's cabin, a beautiful meadow carpeted with wildflowers stretched out before us. The sweeping rock wall that forms the backdrop to Marion Lake loomed in the distance. We were becoming more talkative as the day warmed. No clouds. Turkey, avocado, onion, lettuce, mayonnaise and tomatoes on a whole-wheat roll – lunch on a rock beside the gurgling stream. Two rangers came by and checked our permit.

The last slippery, wet mile of an 8.8-mile day was straight up. Nobody complained – except me. The first day is always the most difficult. Finally over a rise, the lake came into view – a most welcome sight. We dropped our packs and cooled our feet in the clear, cold water.

After scouting all the campsites on the ridge, the first was chosen. It was the flattest and felt the best. Karen and I got the tent up and the bags and pads inside while Roanne cooked dinner which we were almost too tired to eat.

Then a strange thing happened. A couple walked up to us and asked if they could share our campsite. We looked at each other not quite sure they had asked what they did. I told them there were lots of campsites farther on. They looked surprised that we didn't want company and left. I call that the herding instinct. We resumed our dinner feeling intruded upon. There is so little privacy in the world. Isn't that why people go into the mountains?

It turned cold immediately as the sun dropped and we got into our sleeping bags, happy to be on level ground. Roanne fell asleep, exhausted from her late night out the evening before. Karen and I talked into the night. She spoke about her job, and wanting a change; her problems with her father and the decision she had made to live with him after having been on her own for several years; her boyfriend and their life together; art school and the weirdness of the times; her apartment, landlords, bills and the phone company, everyday dealings while those deep, forbidden emotions remained untouched. We had been apart for a long time.

Day 2: It was fun to wake up together and even more fun that it was clear and sunny. With a long day ahead, an early start was a good idea.

Up and out of Marion Lake, past Spearhead Point, Indian Lake, Fossil Mountain and canyons that stretched into Idaho towards the Big Hole Mountains; down and up onto the Death Canyon shelf, through a maze of strange rock formations, wildflowers and unequalled views of the high country. The Teton peaks loomed ahead.

Our favorite waterhole, probably part of a network of subterranean channels, was still gushing forth and Karen filled our bottles while Roanne and I shared some dried apricots and pears.

We headed for Mt. Meek Pass and lunch on the rocks; on to Alaska Basin where we had time for a swim in one of the many small lakes. It was a relief to get our boots off and feel the cool, smooth stones under our hot, sore soles. Roanne was in the water before I had even decided whether I dared; Karen was sitting on a rock, her decision to remain there had been made. I crossed the lake, keeping as much of me out of the water as possible and made it to the rock in the middle where Roanne sat comfortably, coaxing me on. "C'mon, Ma, you can do it."

Ro and me on Death Canyon Shelf

Getting back didn't seem so cold, that is, the wet part of me didn't. My skin tingled as I dried off in the heat of a warm afternoon sun and donned a clean t-shirt – there's nothing like a cold dip in an alpine lake. We draped our wet things over our packs, and refreshed, climbed the last mile to Sunset Lake –our second campsite.

In a clump of trees on a cliff over-looking the lake, turquoise and calm, our tents went up. Mt. Meek was hazy in the distance and the sunlit edges of the basin looked two-dimensional. No clouds. Not too many people. Roanne rubbed our aching shoulders and braided our hair; dinner on a warm rock slab overlooking the lake, watching the sun go down and the sky turn red.

The water was freezing while scrubbing the pots with sand to remove the crumbs of a wonderful meal. We hung our food and climbed into the tent chilled by a slight breeze. Our bags were warm and the ground welcome.

Roanne and Karen played gin rummy while I rested and remembered how close they used to be. When they were young, the two of them were always together, and I could see how happy Ro was to have her sister back. I think it was during the card game "War" that I might have dozed because they were asleep when I awoke.

The stars faded up as the streak in the sky turned from red to purple to slate blue. The darkness swallowed the distant hills. The second day was over. We were all just starting to relax.

I stared at Karen asleep on the other side of Roanne and wondered what really filled her mind. Who is this child? Not a child anymore, although one to me always. We were mother and daughter, not close friends. I'd like to have told her so much but she was never receptive. All those years spent together when I was learning to be a mother, I practiced on my first-born. She didn't look changed. But she was. So was I. There was a painful chasm between us that one day would have to be bridged . . . if we could find the right time. Then, perhaps, we could be friends. The evening darkened, as my mind lit up with a life long ago. Roanne snuggled close unconsciously knowing I needed her love. I think I slept a little.

Day 3: The sun appeared over the wall of Avalanche Canyon and dried the droplets of dew on the tent. It was going to be another clear, warm day.

Two miles up to Hurricane Pass, the trail switchbacked through fields of Indian paintbrush – red, yellow, white and coral – and bluebells brightened the hillside; a barren plateau where everything around us dropped away. Suddenly the Grand pierced the blueness, then the Middle and finally the South Teton. Here, the funniest thing happened on the entire trip.

None of us knew how to set the camera so that all of us could be in a photograph together. We tried balancing it on the wooden sign that marked the altitude and wedged some pebbles under one end to level it. Karen and Roanne placed themselves in the middle of the frame in front of the peaks. I set the lever and listened to it tick. Karen yelled to me but I couldn't move. The ticking stopped but the camera didn't click. Then Karen, who had just bought a Nikon and was becoming interested in photography, gave it a try. She set it up, but didn't quite make it into the picture. Then Roanne and I moved apart so that all she would have to do was run into the space between us. She set it again. The camera started ticking. Karen rushed over and I heard the shutter drop. We burst out laughing and laughed half way down the south fork of Cascade Canyon.

Finally we were relaxed enough for Karen to begin asking questions about our past, questions that might bring clarity to our circumstances and clear the path to love; misunderstood family affairs, unending arguments and disagreements, all those incidents that one never discusses which lead to divorce.

We talked five miles' worth until the junction of the south and north forks and had lunch on a rock, above a rushing stream, in view of a silvery waterfall, and ate in silence. A lot had been said. Outside this canyon it probably wouldn't be remembered. But it was a beginning.

Up the north fork, through an acre of bluebells growing so thick that their hue could be seen long before and after one reached the place where they grew, to Lake Solitude. The three of us had walked too far and passed the end of the camping zone. Roanne and Karen were willing to settle for a slope. I wasn't. So I left them and backtracked with renewed energy. There it was – a flat place next to a trickling brook beside a huge rock for shelter. I called to them but they were out of earshot. So I dropped my pack to reserve the site and trudged back up to where I had left them trying to make their slope level. "You don't settle, Mom, you're determined." A promising note after a long day.

Dinner was a treat and Roanne was the only one who had the energy to make it.

The three of us took turns throwing a rock over a high limb to hang our food, in case of bears – a rock tied to one end of a long cord with the other end fastened to the food bag was pitched over a high branch at just the right distance away from the trunk so that if a bear climbed the tree it couldn't reach the bag. The filled sack was then heaved up to at least twenty feet off the ground and the cord secured around the trunk. We usually had a good laugh performing this task. Either the rock got loose and flew through the air, or the cord got tangled around the branch, or we'd lose the end that we were holding, or the food bag would be too heavy to lift high enough. We finally gave up for another tree. It kept us laughing and the rigors of the day were forgotten.

This is hard for even me to believe. After dinner the three of us decided to walk back up to Lake Solitude for the alpenglow on the Grand. Golden-orange hues lit up the peaks. I sat in solemn awe. No camera.

Nighttime shadows of navy blue accompanied us on the way back. Canyon walls dark. Air still. Nobody but the three of us and the shriek of a hawk.

Another card game and more memories. How do you catch up on ten years in five days? I got my period that night and worried about bears. They can pick up the scent from miles away. But it was the next day I was most apprehensive about – the climb to Indian Paintbrush Divide. From the lake it had looked steep and edgy, a long slice across the mountainside.

This fear of heights was not always part of my existence. When I was seven years old, my parents and I, on our way to Lake Placid, New York, were driving the Whiteface Memorial Highway to the summit. We stopped at a pull-out where my father suddenly picked me up, placed me on the stone wall overlooking the steep gorge and, jokingly, pretended to push me off the wall. I was horrified. He laughed, totally insensitive to my terror. This fear was compounded when, thirteen years ago, I fell twenty-one from a chairlift on Mt. Mansfield in Stowe, Vermont and broke my pelvis. I went up the chair after I was healed but it was never the same.

I told the kids that if the height bothered me they should go
on and I could take a nice, easy walk out of Cascade Canyon and
catch the boat across Jenny Lake for home. It sounded
comforting. "No way, Ma, you're coming with us."

Day 4: The morning dawned bright and clear. Our tent was
spread over a boulder to dry. After eating breakfast and packing
up, we hiked up to Lake Solitude once again, passing the only
field of glacier lilies I had ever seen, to the trail that stretched
across the canyon's north side for two and a half miles and
started the climb. I saw Mica Lake for the first time, a tiny, green
body of water at the foot of a glacier high up in the canyon wall.

The first set of switchbacks brought incomparably beautiful
views of the entire range. Looking down onto Hurricane Pass
and the south and north forks of Cascade Canyon was a thrill.
The trail flattened along a ridge between some stunted
evergreens, then switchbacked to the top. Snow patches melted
into turquoise rivulets that gurgled past and down the other side

Karen, Roanne and Me on Paintbrush Divide,

into a tiny, murky pond. The sign on the top was marked 10,700 feet. A guy laden with camera equipment did us a favor and took our picture.

Lunch on a rock – a cold wind forced us to change to sweaters and sweat pants – while sitting quietly enjoying the altitude. We could see into Moran and Leigh Canyons to the north, the Sawtooths to the west, and to the east, the Gros Ventres and Wind Rivers.

The switchbacks on this side of the divide were the steepest I had ever encountered. Loose rocks slid on our descent into the upper part of Paintbrush Canyon. Traversing a treacherous snowfield, kicking footsteps into it, Roanne's hand was the reassurance I needed to get across. Jackson Lake, its islands, and the east edge of Leigh Lake came into view while Jackson Hole stretched out in front of us as we rounded a bend and descended to deep, bluish-green Holly Lake at the foot of Mt. Woodring. A readymade site appeared and the three of us collapsed on the ground, glad to be off our feet. The girls set up camp and walked down to the water's edge. I crawled into the tent and didn't move the rest of the afternoon.

I was more than tired. It had been a long, emotionally exhausting day – not only because the hiking had been all up and down – I had been worried about the climb to the Divide. Those situations seem to take it out of me. I'm not as carefree as my daughters who were raised in the mountains rather than in a city like myself. I'm just a frightened child sometimes.

The tent sides billowed gently and kept me cool. For the first time on our trip, I opened my book. Gin rummy in the sun between the girls took up the last rays and the evening stillness settled in, disturbed only by a slight breeze, refreshing on our sunburned skin.

We were almost sad thinking about the walk out tomorrow – a sadness mixed with excitement that I knew would be short-lived at seeing and hearing the first car or truck on the highway.

These trips were precious. We didn't have to deal with the normal distractions of everyday life, being too busy taking care of ourselves and one other – keeping dry and warm, well-fed,

Indian Paintbrush Divide

a clean camp – surviving. No demands, no appointments, no
time schedules, no bills, no deadlines, no messages, no mail. It
was easier in the mountains. And of course my beautiful
daughters were close which always filled my heart with love.

Day 5: The morning came too quickly. We didn't talk much while packing up, not caring to put the sleeping bags in their sacks or anything in its proper place. Our toilet paper was vanishing and rationing ourselves was in order for the last day.

Six and a half miles out – I was glad to be going down this canyon and not up. A rushing creek, here and there a nodding calypso, one of the most dainty of mountain flowers, fireweed, an occasional wild rose, and a family of moose that skittered away at our approach. The trail, heavy with huckleberries, entered deep, somber woods that skirted the shores of Leigh Lake and dropped finally to its outlet.

After a quick snack on the bridge, another mile brought us to noisy civilization, the String Lake parking lot. We hitched a ride in the back of somebody's pickup and bumped along stopping at all the tourist spots on the way to Moose, a tiny community at the entrance to the Park on the banks of the Snake River.

A cold beer and a telephone. Marty was glad to hear my voice and would be around as soon as he could drive the nine miles to meet us. Burnt and brown. You could tell the three of us had been away for a few days. We had that wild, mountain look – and smell.

The weather had made this trip – no storms, no lightning, nothing but joy. Our hearts were warm, our eyes were clear, and there was a lot of love between us.

"Wilderness is where nature is free to exist as it did in ages past, self-willed and untrammeled, and where we are free to experience a feeling of solitude and self-reliance found nowhere else."

Wilderness Watch

IV

Lake Solitude

June 1987:

Inclement weather didn't force me to say no when Roanne had two days off work and wanted to go for a hike. It was 4:00 p.m. and raining when the boat across Jenny Lake finally dropped us at Cascade Canyon. With our packs, food for a couple of days, and her Nepali flash cards (a vocabulary trainer to learn Nepali), we made a beeline for a campsite before the clouds dumped more rain in the valley. Lake Solitude would look good in the rain . . . I guessed.

Hordes of hikers coming down the canyon stared at us going the other way. Determined to get to our favorite spot before too late, it was fortunate that the four and a half miles to the forks were straight, easy walking. A ranger along the way answered my question. Yes, there were reports of bears, a sow and two cubs and a large bruin wandering around, also lots of moose.

"C'mon, Ma." Roanne didn't care, and didn't want to be bothered with me caring either. Halfway up the north fork our familiar site near a stream surrounded by trees in the shelter of a huge boulder materialized. It took minutes to set up our tent and cook dinner – couscous, mixed vegetables, gravy and a piece of Randy's chocolate cake. Randy, an avid hiker/backpacker, was the boss of the bakery where Roanne worked. While hanging our food another ranger stopped to check our permit. No, there hadn't been any bears around, not for days. Maybe I would get some sleep.

We even had time to run up the rest of the two and a half miles to Lake Solitude to see the alpenglow on the west side of the Grand. It was worth the whole trip – as always. The light was fading as our tent came into view. Tired and wet, our bags were more than welcome. Roanne was sleepy but I wasn't, so I coaxed her to stay up and talk. She studied her flash cards with me until dark. About 9:30 p.m.

No rain. No noise. Nothing stirred. She was asleep. I had my trusty flashlight in the tent pocket beside me, my Calms, tiny green homeopathic pills to help me relax in the wilds, and my book that I couldn't concentrate on. I thought of Roanne's upcoming trip to Nepal, a place in my dreams where she was actually going to live for six months. It was far off but approaching quickly. There was still a lot more time to walk in the wilderness. She was my best partner and I, hers.

Ro had started college at World College West, a small, private school in Petaluma, California where the students could spend their second year at one of three places – China, Mexico or Nepal. For her first year she had studied Nepali, the language and culture, in order to prepare for this monumental adventure.

"Aren't you sleeping yet, Ma?" She turned over and closed her eyes again. A slight drizzle on the tent was comforting. I could hear the pleasant trickling of the nearby stream. Alone in the canyon.

I don't remember sleeping but when I awoke it was still dark, although there was some light coming from somewhere. I looked out of the tent and could see the outlines of the canyon walls, the peaks framed in the doorway. As I stared outside, Roanne, warm beside me, stirred and snuggled close. She wasn't up yet.

The nights give me time to think. About all sorts of things – the books I want to write, stones I want to carve, feelings I have for this daughter, memories of my other two girls, the place where I live, and the wilderness I love.

It was starting to turn grey, soft raindrops on the rainfly. Dry and warm inside, moist and sweet-smelling outside. I dozed comfortably.

Day 2: We opened our eyes together and listened to the rain; both of us loved being here and looked forward to breakfast while talking about college, Nepal, dear friends, her sisters, and us – how being apart for so long was going to feel. It was then that a decision was made to keep track of our letters by numbering them because many kids returned never having received any.

I spread the rainfly over a huge boulder to dry while she prepared breakfast – granola, milk, a bagel and tea. With nowhere to go, nothing to do and only a seven-mile walk out, there was no rush. It was close to 11:00 a.m. when the first noisy hikers were heard coming up to Lake Solitude. Perfume passed us on the trail and, grimacing at the intrusion after a long, peaceful night, a look of understanding between us.

The flowers were especially brilliant after the rain and I decided to pick one of each kind and press them when I got home. I had never picked wildflowers in the park or the wilderness and I did it against my better judgment. But it was so much more accurate to mix my inks for my stonecut prints from the actual flower rather than a slide or photograph. So I discreetly collected a few samples against Roanne's gentle disapproval – Indian paintbrush, Lewis monkeyflower, mountain bluebell, sticky geranium, glacier lily, alpine forget-me-not and a harebell. My colorful specimens were in my hot, little hand when a ranger unexpectedly came up from behind. Of all times . . . he sternly reprimanded me for picking wildflowers in the park. I told him that I never picked wildflowers in the park, I knew better and that I was an artist and needed the real thing to draw from and . . . he lectured me, "what if everybody just picked one of each?" . . . and I promised I would never do it again. I felt awkward and embarrassed. I thought for a moment he was going to cite me. Lucky for me that he didn't.

Roanne looked at me in that motherly way that I used to look at her when I caught her hand in the cookie jar (actually candy jar in our house).

Another hike behind us, a few more days spent in our summer together. She knew her Nepali by heart. She was doing well. I was doing . . . okay.

Indian Paintbrush, Lewis monkeyflowers, mountain bluebells, sticky geranium, glacier lilies, alpine forget-me-nots, harebells

V

Static Peak

July 1987:

The weather was formidable when we decided to use Roanne's two days off work and climb Static Peak. But I was hesitant. It was getting on in the day and raining sporadically. Why leave a toasty, dry home for the wet, muddy trails in the Park?

She didn't say a word and because of her quiet enthusiasm, we left finally, at almost 2:00 p.m., for the boat across Jenny Lake.

It didn't take long to reach the forks. Up the south fork, lush with wildflowers, and as our climb continued, their colors became more intense. Charged with excitement and still dry, a decision to forego our Avalanche Canyon permit and head over the pass to Sunset Lake was made. Dark clouds coursed overhead as the switchbacks started up the headwall. A rainbow, mauve, turquoise and pink, suddenly stretched across the mountainside, leaning up against the peaks. How special!

Up and up and suddenly the top was just ahead with an unsurpassed view of Idaho and Battleship Mountain to the west, Mt. Meek to the south, the forks of Cascade Canyon to the north, and a rich, blue sky above! It's a great place, the top of the world.

Being on Hurricane Pass gives one a more objective view of things. The Grand, Middle and South Tetons, seemingly only an arm's length to the east, were draped in billowing clouds, peeking in and out as the storm moved northeast toward Jackson Hole where Marty was watching and thinking of us in the rain. Thunder rumbled and lightning flashed all around us. The rainbow had faded but there were blue skies ahead while descending to Sunset Lake. At 5:30 p.m. our tent was up. I was ready for bed before dinner.

A leisure walk around the lake gave Ro a chance to go swimming in the freezing water. I went in up to my knees and could barely breathe. I envy her being able to do that. The sound of a flute from the cliff above the lake accompanied us back to our tent – almost an intrusion – but peaceful along with a few voices of campers tuned to city life.

The setting sun left an orange strip across the horizon which gradually faded as we crawled into our sleeping bags, happy to be horizontal. There's nothing like stretching out after a forced, thirteen-mile march.

Hikers were still arriving. It had cooled off considerably and being in rather than out made us happy. The sky was darkening and stars appeared, a few at a time. They got bright and then brighter as the sky turned light purple. The Milky Way stretched across the horizon. Her Nepali flashcards came out with another perfect score and she talked about a fairytale land in the East across the great Pacific; about how high the Himalayas were and how exciting it would be to see them.

Another few months and Ro would be on her way; still sure about going; unquestionably definite. There was no changing her mind although I had tried with all kinds of bribes – a VW bug, money in her pocket, anything I could think of, but there was a tone in her voice and I gave up. I was actually impressed that she was going on such an exciting adventure, but apprehensive. She's my kid. I like her close. I don't feel like her mother. She's my friend. I think she's asleep. I nudge her to stay up with me. She says she'll try but I know she's gone.

I like it when it's light and the landscape just barely discernible. I try to relax. My legs are still walking up and down, my muscles, warm and tingling. Raindrops. A passing cloud. I watch it go by. Another approaches. That light pitter-patter on the tent, then quiet again. I try to read but can't concentrate. There's so much up here that fills my senses. And I'm tired. It had been a long afternoon since leaving the boat dock and here we were at Sunset Lake. How unexpected.

I love to be able to change my mind like I did today. It gives me a feeling of impermanence. Walking makes me feel alive and healthy. Visually, there's nothing like it. If I keep walking I'll never grow old. So I'll keep walking. With Roanne. She keeps me young. I don't quit as fast. I walk farther and more briskly. Her energy mixes with mine and between us a positive force is created that benefits both.

I think I dozed a bit because the sky was lightening. The sound of soft rain made me warm and comfortable. Ro stirred. Silence. Again raindrops. Another passing cloud. The sky was dull. Well, what of it? Waking up in our tent at Sunset Lake – how bad could it be? Since we were getting out today it didn't matter whether we were wet or dry.

Day 2: After breakfast we packed between clouds, and, keeping our ponchos out, started up the ridge to Alaska Basin and Static Peak, wading through vibrant fields of flowers. At the top of the hill the trail traversed the eastern edge of the basin, along the foot of Buck Mountain, over a divide and towards another. Confused momentarily as to where the trail around Static was . . . no, it couldn't be that peak in the distance where we were headed. Even Ro was startled. I told her I didn't want to go up that high. But there was no turning back. It was too late in the morning to make another decision. She was going to have her hands full.

Making steady progress up the steep, sheer slope, the trail suddenly stopped, a rockfall barring our way. Which way to go? What to do? Another switchback. I didn't like this at all! Higher and higher, continuing along narrow ledges of crumbling rock until finally at 10,800 feet the two of us entered another world – Static Peak Divide, a plateau that rose five hundred feet to its peak and dropped off to nothing on the other side.

I was nervous. She knew I was nervous. Why do I put myself through this? It said for hardy hikers. Well, I consider myself a hardy hiker, but not nuts.

South of Static Peak Divide, the trail was narrow with long, bottomless drop-offs and I felt exposed. I knew it was eight miles down to the trailhead at Death Canyon, five of those miles got you from the trailhead to the ranger's cabin at the opening of the canyon. So there were three miles left of this.

"Watch my boots, Ma."

Good idea. Then I didn't have to think about the yawning nothingness on my left. I watched her boots as they moved forward. I didn't even want to lift my feet to take a step. She led me across the narrow path and around the first switchback, my pack brushing against the side of the mountain. Hopefully that would be the worst of it. But it continued. Being on the inside of the mountain was a bit of a reprieve. At the end of that section, the next steep, unnerving switchback loomed ahead, again with us on the outside hanging off the edge. I didn't look down often. In fact, never, until the trail widened just enough to get off the edge. I did feel the void out of the corners of my eyes but I could breathe again. Hopefully the worst was over. That's what I mean when I say she's got patience. She is gentle with me, comforting and encouraging.

"I know this was a bad one, Ma."

The rest of the descent, long and wet, was devoid of pitfalls. I considered us lucky, actually, because there was thunder and lightning back in the basin and only rain up ahead. The sky opened up.

Down through the trees, walking back and forth across the mountainside for three miles. Our feet were sloshing around in our boots and we couldn't have been wetter when the bottom and the ranger's cabin finally came into view.

Lunch among the dripping trees – sardines, cheese, whole-wheat rolls, carrot and celery sticks.

It kept raining and the two of us kept walking through Death Canyon heading for Phelps Lake and a lift to our car parked at the Jenny Lake boat dock. Would some kind soul let us into the back of their pickup the way we looked? There were two hikers behind us.

After climbing the three switchbacks to the overlook, a stop to have a fig was essential while dropping our waterlogged packs and ponchos, stripping down to dry off and wrapping our bodies in warm t-shirts and shorts. Our sweatpants had stretched about ten inches and were difficult to drag any further.

A little way down the trail Roanne realized that I didn't have my poncho on the top of my pack. I didn't care about it and certainly wasn't going back. But she did while I waited on the trail. A couple had picked it up and left it on a rock.

Would we dare ask them for a lift in our condition? Roanne joked that they probably had a new Subaru and wouldn't even consider it. Well, they did have a new Subaru but were almost as messy as us! Climbing into the back the four of us bumped along over the rutted, dirt road towards the highway.

They had noticed us yesterday in Cascade Canyon walking as if we had somewhere to go. They were on a two-month trip visiting the National Parks and were on their way to Glacier and points west. Yes, we lived in Jackson Hole and never had to leave.

The two of us were dropped off at our van after they gave us their address and instructions for a wonderful four days in the Grand Canyon where he had been a guide. Wouldn't that be fun to do on some dry day in the distant future? After Nepal. Roanne drove home. It's great to have a kid with a driver's license after a hard hike in the mountains.

"Leaving nothing but footprints.
Take nothing but photos.
Kill nothing but time.
Keep nothing but memories."

Leave No Trace,
Center for Outdoor Ethics

VI

The Wind Rivers

August 1987:

After leaving the Jackson Hole Valley, heading south past
Hoback Junction, the temperature dropped. It was 6 a.m. Ninety
miles to Pinedale and fourteen more to the Elkhart Park
entrance, one of the western gates to the Wind River Range, the
most inaccessible wilderness in Wyoming. Roanne, myself and
Susan were going for a six-day backpacking trip. She, an avid
hiker who visited Jackson Hole almost yearly, found our gallery
in Jackson's Crabtree Corner, fell in love with our artwork and
kept returning to purchase more. We became friends. Susan had
had an operation three months ago, had recuperated fully and
was still up for the trip we had talked about when she was last
out West. None of us had ever hiked in the Winds.

Had she not come along, Roanne and I would have headed
into the Tetons again. Living with them in our backyard was
reason to never go anywhere else. Randy, a guy with whom
Roanne baked during a summer job, had been telling her about
the Winds for two years. He didn't even bother hiking in the
Tetons anymore. It was too crowded. Having looked at this
southern range from the Amphitheater/Surprise Lakes trail it
was always snow-covered when there was no snow on the Teton
peaks. So we bought Finis Mitchell's book and the geological
survey topographical maps and planned a hike.

The Wind River Range stretches a little over one hundred
miles between South Pass and Togwotee Pass, has the highest
peak in the state, 13,804-foot Gannett Peak, and over two
thousand lakes, a fisherman's paradise. Between the north

and south boundaries of the Winds, no road crosses or even penetrates the hundred-mile crest. It is entirely wilderness.

8:00 a.m. It was cold at the Elkhart parking lot. I felt a knot of excitement in the pit of my stomach. This was a first for all of us. I wondered how we would fare together.

8:20 a.m. found us on the trail after the last bites of an overly ripened peach and a visit to the outhouse. With fifteen miles to Island Lake, two days walking at high elevations continuously, I hoped Susan, who came from the Midwest, would be okay. Somebody had said there were No bears! in the Winds. Maybe I would get some sleep. Being above timberline most of the time made me happy. "It's apt to snow at anytime in this country." We were prepared.

The trail was wet and sloppy. It had snowed on and off for the last eleven days, a couple, glad to be on their way out, told us. There was about four to five inches at the start. I hated to get my new boots muddy so I picked my steps carefully, searching for dry ground.

A short way in we peeled off outer layers. Warm and windy. Passed tiny, snow-rimmed lakes, crossed expansive meadows ringed with trees and got a glimpse of distant peaks. The sun burned bright between billowy, white clouds that sailed by, not too far overhead. After four miles, a sign for the Miller Lake cutoff appeared and I could finally pinpoint our whereabouts on the map. The first miles were on another quadrangle which I didn't have.

Through a glade, into some woods, up a shallow, rocky ravine and around a bend – there they were – the snowy peaks of the Continental Divide stretching across the horizon. We stood aghast, our hearts pounding, both from excitement and a lack of oxygen.

At Photographers Point a group of hikers were sitting on a rock taking in the view over lunch and, coveting our privacy, we continued on, deciding to take some shots on the way out. At Ekland Lake the trail forked, left to the Island Lake country and Titcomb Basin where we were heading, and right to Cook Lakes, which could provide us with a loop on our way out in about a week.

Continuing north around Barbara Lake, the snow had started to melt, turning the trail to mud. Lunch on some rocks near Hobbs Lake gave us a chance to quietly look around at this strange country – hilly and panoramic.

After a satisfying meal and helping each other lift our incredibly heavy packs onto our backs, the three of us pressed on, wondering how much farther it was to Seneca Lake and our first campsite. We crossed a few streams – no bridges – and climbed a strenuous slope which brought us to the steep, rocky, western shore of a huge, beautiful body of water in a glaciated area dotted with scrub trees and Mt. Lester in the background.

We split up and searched for a campsite but could find nothing and continued around the lake. Still nothing. Our packs were getting heavier with each step and our energy was running out. The landscape was soggy. Every time a flat spot appeared, it was too wet, too rocky or too close to the trail. Already out of sight of the lake, much to our disappointment, it was late afternoon when finally Roanne called from ahead. "I've got one!" Our packs slid to the dry, almost level ground for the last time; changed into warm clothes and set up camp while Roanne cooked dinner: couscous, mixed vegetables and gravy, half a bagel each and some peppermint tea, using Susan's wonderful stainless steel camping pots.

As the last rays of the sun disappeared, it turned cold. After hanging the food, just to be sure, the three of us climbed into our tent. Not having planned to sleep together this was a bit of a shock and something for us to get over. Roanne and I preferred to sleep alone. That's why we brought two tents.

To lie horizontal was sheer happiness. The clouds dissolved and the sky darkened slowly while we talked about the day, wondering how many miles were covered and how different this place was from the Tetons – a lot less crowded although some campers setting up late could be heard. Susan and Roanne fell asleep immediately.

About 2 a.m. I felt the call of nature. As I unzipped the tent door and stepped out into the night I noticed a myriad of white spots on the ground at my feet and on the rocks and grass around me. In fact the entire area was covered. I looked up at the sky. There was no blackness, no detectable Milky Way, just a luminescence of stars. No single identifiable star body or planet but a brilliant lacy web of radiance. The entire curvature of the sky shimmered and was reflected on the Earth under my feet. Crouched in the bushes at 10,400 feet I noticed my toes spotted with tiny circles of light. I looked up again. Trillions of stars shone forming a lustrous grid. I had never seen anything like this before.

It was very cold and I shivered in my sleeping bag while watching the sky. I listened and changed position and looked up again. It was mesmerizing. Something different was definitely happening in the heavens.

Day 2: 5:35 a.m. The stars were gone. Imperceptible light. I hardly sleep at this altitude and when I do, it's sporadic. I dozed until 7:00 a.m. The sun, shining in a crystal clear, blue sky warmed the inside of the tent and our early morning feelings were positive. Snug and cozy. Sleepy eyes. Good morning greetings. Smiles. The ground was still icy and I spread the rainfly over a warm rock to dry.

Our huge bundle of food hanging in a tree looked like a dead body and reminded me of an old western movie. Hot ramen for breakfast and a decision to save the other half of our first bagel (we had allotted two per person for the trip) for after dinner tonight. After brushing our teeth, washing and rearranging the weight in our packs we heaved them onto our sore shoulders. They slid easily into yesterday's grooves.

Everybody who had arrived late last night were just getting up as the three of us picked our way around some wet spots and met up with the trail. Water was filtered at Little Seneca Lake and our bottles filled. Parts of the trail were submerged causing us to climb to higher ground to get around the lake. At the junction of the Highline Trail, the main route that follows close to timberline along the entire west side of the range, we headed north up a series of switchbacks to a high saddle. The frosty peaks of the Continental Divide suddenly appeared on the horizon.

After waiting until our hearts stopped pounding and our breathing returned to normal, some dried figs and apricots were shared while contemplating the sinuous trail that disappeared through a notch over another rise in the distance. The Indian Pass Trail led us to Island Lake, a spectacular body of water at the foot of the Divide, with a broken isle of rocks strewn down its middle. Roanne ran ahead to secure a spot she had read about in Finis Mitchell's book while I descended slowly, not wanting to lose the panoramic perspective. She was perched on top of a boulder pointing to a small patch of trees on a knoll overlooking the lake. How perfect. Two whole days would be spent here, exploring.

The tents went up and lunch was out instantaneously: smoked oysters, avocado (our mouths dropped open as Ro pulled it out of her pack), a green pepper, carrots, rice cakes, soy cheese and whole wheat rolls – a grand spread.

It was mid-afternoon and the sun was high overhead. I think Susan wanted to relax but chose to join us when Ro and I decided to hike up to 12,120-foot Indian Pass on the Divide; no packs, just an afternoon stroll, saving the whole of the next day for Titcomb Basin. With some dried fruit in our pockets, Ro hung a water bottle from her waist, and the three of us climbed into Indian Basin, a beautiful, desolate limestone bowl – all pink and beige – and wandered into a rocky world of warm tones and polychromatic peaks. The sun was hot and I could feel my skin roasting. Susan had a headache. After taking pictures of one another, she turned back and Ro and I headed towards the pass and into more snow. Some footsteps appeared, probably left from the NOLS (National Outdoor Leadership School) group who had passed us back at Seneca Lake, and continued over a rushing stream. Across a huge snowfield, along the edge of a tiny lake, they suddenly disappeared and we built cairns to landmark our return.

Me and Ro, Indian Basin

The peaks were unfamiliar and without a book for identification mental notes were taken to look them up at home.

The Divide towered before us; up a steep chute until the snow got too deep and dangerous to proceed without ice axes. Retracing our steps, glad to having marked the way, a promise was made to return next year. Our spirits high, our boots wet, we emerged once more into summertime. It was fun for the two of us to be alone.

At 10,600 feet, a deep, tranquil, turquoise pool enticed Roanne. "C'mon, Ma!" Off with her clothes, into the icy water, out of the icy water, and on with her clothes! She had it down from her days in Mendocino when the beach was full of people and she and her friends went for a swim at lunchtime or after class. No towels or wet suits and in a hurry. I got as far in as my toes. "Uh-uh, not this time." A cool breeze kept us dry while walking back slowly . . . clear skies, rocks across a creek, a waterfall, a distant mountain range, infinity, and the cutoff to Titcomb Basin, shielded by a narrow, rocky gorge. Until tomorrow.

On our return Susan told us that a ranger had come by and asked her to move. The tent was in view of the trail. We could stay the night but had to leave in the morning. She had told him about this spot in Mitchell's book and all he could say was that Finis was an old man and that was a long time ago. There were rules in the wilderness. I have always thought of myself as a conscientious, disciplined camper and I was aggravated. It would have been nice to settle in for two days without moving.

Our boots and socks were spread out to dry in the remaining heat while we complained about bureaucracy all through dinner, and a decision was made to drop the tents to the ground out of view during the day and write a letter to the Bridger-Teton Wilderness Headquarters. If there were rules to follow, why not post them!

Susan fell asleep while Roanne and I talked and giggled softly, trying not to wake her. The sky darkened and turned a washed-out navy blue. No wind, quiet and cold. A candle was lit for gin rummy. It was difficult to stay covered and warm without dropping our cards. Ro complained that she could see my hand. Gin for me, gin for her, a few more games and I could see Roanne's eyes starting to close. "Okay, Ma, one more game."

I lay awake for a long time. My muscles stretched, blood rushed in, and I started to relax. I'd like to meet this ranger and give him a piece of my . . . calm . . . tranquil . . . quiet mind.

Day 3: I must have been sleeping because I became aware of the dawn suddenly. The sun was shining on the other side of the valley, its warmth inching across the landscape. Sue was asleep so Roanne and I walked over to a bright spot, sat on a warm rock and had some granola and milk. The icy ground softened around our feet. Sue got up and had her breakfast while Ro and I spread everything out to dry. As the sun rose in a blue, cloudless sky a discussion about our weird, vivid dreams ensued.

Our minds were made up. I thought it would be a good idea to move. Susan felt the same way. Roanne thought not to. She's such a rebel. I love her. But she was outnumbered so, assembling our stuff, hanging our packs off of one shoulder and dragging the half-folded tent to another spot hidden by a huge boulder, we pitched the tents, stashed our gear, packed a lunch, and headed for Titcomb Basin.

After crossing a wide, rushing stream carefully and picking our way over a soggy meadow, a climb through a narrow passageway dropped us into the adjacent valley. What came next was a visually perfect piece of art that took my breath away. I was quite unprepared for the full beauty of the scene – a sculpted valley of stone, embracing a chain of three viridian alpine lakes on rising ledges, encircled by the jagged snowy peaks of the Continental Divide – Fremont, Mt. Sacajawea, Mt. Helen, Mt. Warren, Dinwoody, they went on; crossed rock-studded, tundra-like ground, wet almost everywhere. Wild-flowers were still in bloom including a succulent rose crown I've never seen before.

Suddenly a sonic boom stopped us in our spots. The rocks seemed to shudder. It was unnerving. Continuing to the north end of the three-mile long basin, a calm place for lunch couldn't be found because of the cold wind funneling down the valley. A deep crevice in a boulder field under which a creek tumbled into the middle lake provided shelter.

Susan seemed uncomfortable – the cold, the wind, a high altitude headache and we started back. Two climbers passed and asked if that was our tent on the knoll at Island Lake. They thought us lucky to get that spot. After telling them we had been asked to move, they smiled at each other and said that that "busybody," as they called the ranger whom they knew well, was living up to his name. Our aggravation at having to move camp wasn't totally unfounded.

At the first lake Roanne and I left the trail and climbed higher, I with my camera for a bird's eye view and she, like a mountain goat glued to the sides of huge boulders, to fly. With all of one rock-climbing lesson behind her, she tested her skills and made me crazy. I've learned to allow her her space and keep relatively calm. It's not always easy.

"C'mon, Ma, it's great up here." Susan passed and we ran to catch up.

The air was electric, the water crystalline, the earth warm, and there was fire in our hearts. This was God's country. James Hilton wrote about it, Edward Abbey lived in it, and we had just walked through it. Reluctantly climbing through the gorge that concealed this creation I stepped away slowly, looking back, not wanting to let it go, a vision so glorious it brought tears to my eyes. Ro and I looked at one another knowing we'd return.

While descending to Island Lake, the "busybody" came up behind us. I told him that I was upset and he apologized. He said that the prime objective was to keep this a wilderness area. Hikers shouldn't see tents near trails. Visual impact. They were trying to educate the public. He could cite us if we wouldn't move. Okay, I could understand all of that. Then cordon off the area, I suggested. It looked used, it was used all the time. He said that would make it look like a park instead of wilderness. He had a good argument, but why did he have to pick on us? He was sorry; he hoped I would understand. After such an apology, what can one say.

Back at camp, Susan decided to take a bath in a secluded inlet just around the hill from our campsite. Her head had stopped throbbing and she felt more relaxed. Roanne and I, charged with energy and overwhelmed by our latest adventure, headed for the sandy beach at the other end of the lake that we had passed on our way in.

After washing a few things and spreading them over warm rocks to dry, Ro plunged into the water and swam towards the middle of the lake. "C'mon, Ma, you'll love it." I was in the mood. I ran in after her, ducked up to my neck, splashed around and dashed out into her waiting towel. I tugged at my clinging t-shirt, dropped my shorts, hoping there was nobody around, and, refreshed, put on clean, dry clothes and collapsed on our one towel. My skin tingled, wet and cool, brushed by a slight breeze. The two of us stared across the lake into a blue sky at a clump of clouds sitting on the horizon. A gull flew by. Birds chirped in the trees. Gurgling water. Stillness.

Sandy beach at Island Lake

Following her natural curiosity, Ro climbed the hill behind us to see where the creek came from while I stretched out, digging my toes into the warm sand and running my fingers through it. I relished this time alone.

The ranger strolled by again on his rounds and I asked about Lester Pass and Cook Lakes where Randy fished. He said the Pass was a gradual climb and the lakes only about four miles or so past that. He drew a picture in the sand and suggested a campsite. With three more days to go, having gotten to this point more quickly than anticipated and based on his information, which I imparted to Roanne, a decision was made to talk it over with Susan and see how she felt. It would give us a chance to see more of the country by making a loop rather than walking out the same way we had come in. Another quick dip to get the sand off left Ro shrieking with laughter as I desperately tried to keep my bottom out of view and the towel around it dry.

Back at our site Susan was getting out the cooking pots. Roanne started dinner while I shielded the stove from the wind that had just picked up. A change to wool hats and gloves, sweatpants over long underwear, sweaters and down vests was necessary when the sun disappeared; dinner in a warm tent was relaxing after an exquisite day.

Roanne's cup was missing. The three of us walked over the area between our first campsite and this one hoping to pick it up. Back at camp it suddenly popped out of her pack. Hot peppermint tea and a piece of our second raisin bagel was a treat while tucked into our sleeping bags and, lo and behold, an apple from Ro's pack.

Another night was upon us. Susan went to sleep while Ro and I played gin rummy and talked about her upcoming trip to Nepal, and our new find, the Wind Rivers. The last sliver of a moon shone. She went to sleep and I prepared to "ground": to run (balance) my energy so that I could become calm and open my mind to the energy of the moment. I had hours to think. I was physically spent but my senses were alert.

I think sometimes people find it hard to be with Ro and me. We're always hugging and kissing and I play with her curls to the point of making her crazy. I wonder if Susan is bothered, if she feels like a third party. I hope not.

I could hear Roanne's steady breathing next to me. All that could be seen of her was a mass of blond ringlets. I played with them until she turned over and groaned.

What do I want to do with my life? What makes me happy? Living with space around me, fewer neighbors, more trees, and only the sound of natural things; the need to feel visually secluded seems important. It's called wilderness. The Tetons are beautiful and the Winds are remote; days to get into the country and miles to walk. The feeling of being up high makes my cells vibrate at a different frequency. I have more energy, breathe more easily and see more clearly. Colors are more vibrant. Excitement is high-pitched. Mediocrity doesn't dwell in wilderness. Freedom and danger do.

The shades of night dissolved into grey; another day was about to dawn. No clouds.

Day 4: Susan said okay to our plan. Because it was some-what of a climb, her weight except clothes, sleeping bag and pad was split between Roanne and myself. Having had a serious operation a few months ago, she needed all her energy for the ascent to 11,000 feet. She's had a headache at 10,600 feet so we proceeded slowly, having decided to turn back if she was uncomfortable. And according to the ranger it wasn't that far or difficult.

Back across the basin, descending to Julie Lake where the Highline Trail continued south to the lake country, an elderly gray-haired woman, wrinkled by the winds of the wilderness, carrying a heavy load passed us. Her clothes looked like she'd been on the trail for weeks. I would have liked to have known her age but she was so intent on her walking, I didn't want to interrupt her reverie. Roanne looked back at me. I smiled. She smiled. Both of us had the same thought. That'll be me thirty years from now and her in fifty years. She left us with strong, warm feelings of respect.

Stopped for some dried fruit and filtered water for our bottles. After a gradual climb to a basin with a number of beautiful lakes (I counted nine), the trail headed for its high point, 11,080-foot Lester Pass. This is the one that had worried us; proceeding slowly and resting often. Every time we thought we were there, there was farther to go. Finally Roanne, who had disappeared up ahead, waved, indicating she was at the top. The last few switchbacks were conquered. Hallelujah! Gradual, the ranger had said? My foot!

Somebody had told us that on a clear day you could see the Tetons. Well, we couldn't but a magnificent view of a far-flung panorama of tremendous mountains clad with eternal snow, emerald lakes and green slopes filled our senses. It was exhilarating to be up so high. The sun was hot, a gentle wind blew. It didn't take long to find a sheltered pocket up against some tumbled boulders for lunch although the three of us were almost too excited to eat. With our boots and packs off, we just relaxed, staring into space, everything below us. I could feel the sun burning my eyelids and pulled my bandanna down over the frames of my sunglasses. The backs of my hands were burnt and I covered them carefully after spreading vitamin E on them.

We gazed about – 360 degrees – and stayed for a while figuring there wasn't too far to go. Roanne, hardly hungry, bounced from boulder to boulder until she was so high we could barely see her. Susan wondered where she got it – all that energy. She's nineteen, that's where.

Started down into the forest-clad valley of Cook Lakes. The ground had dried up after three full days of intense sunshine and walking was easier. The trail suddenly came to a dead end. It just stopped. The dotted line on the map stopped as well. Staring across the wide, tumbling creek, the rough wooden sign that must be where the trail forked to Cook Lakes could barely be made out.

Off with our boots, on with our flip-flops and into the water. Roanne carried her pack over and came back for Susan's. The three of us waded across, knee-deep in rushing water on slippery rocks, balancing our heavy loads. This was the wilderness – no bridges, no mileage markers, just a topo map and a prayer. Isn't that how the Indians did it? And they didn't have maps.

The lakes were about a half-mile upstream. We stumbled onto the campsite Randy had told Roanne about: an outdoor fireplace with cut wood and kindling in the shelter of an immense boulder, a log on which to sit and watch the fire, a flat tent area padded with fragrant evergreen boughs, a gurgling mountain stream, a waterfall, and a lake. Suddenly all of us had the same urge. We tore off our clothes and jumped into the water with screams of pleasure – children again without a care in the world. The water was crystal clear and cold. Roanne crossed the stream and dove off a rock into a deep, green pool. I played in a shallow pool and Susan went up towards the falls to wash her hair. After scrubbing our clothes and frolicking in the setting sun, the three of us wrapped ourselves in towels and relaxed on the rocks, rejoicing after a long, hard day – about eleven or twelve miles. The ranger who had caused us such anxiety about moving our tent didn't know what he was talking about and spoke about educating the public! Give a guy a uniform and a little authority . . . perhaps he should be a bit more concerned about educating himself. He certainly had led us astray. We made it but we might not have.

Roanne and me at Cook Lakes

How fresh I felt – thin, vibrant, excited and hungry! I started a fire while Roanne cooked dinner. She loved Susan's pots, so different from our old, aluminum utensils. We all sat on the log while eating and watched the crackling fire. The sun was setting. Clouds stretched across the sky, the first we'd seen in days. Sue crawled into her bag and Roanne and I were left in front of the fire, too luxurious to leave. All that could be heard was the waterfall and an occasional jet. I guess they have to get across the Divide somewhere.

More clouds moved in, the sky deepened and the woods turned dark. Reluctantly, the two of us climbed into our bags, listened to the sounds while gazing out of the tent for as long as we could see, then played some gin rummy, each winning a few games. It didn't seem as cold as it had been, but then we were at a lower altitude.

Roanne looked so sweet lying next to me. She was dreaming, so I nudged her gently. She smiled sleepily, gave me a goodnight kiss and rolled over, off to some other plane or perhaps past lifetime. I "grounded" and tried to relax. I wasn't particularly tired.

A strangeness had crept into our relationship with Susan. She had thanked us for carrying her load, but accused me of being goal-orientated because a schedule had to be met; how many days in, where to be each day to get out on time, (having told our loved ones when to expect us), having enough food for the trip. I hadn't remembered her remark until now and knew I would eventually have to deal with my feelings. I think there is a difference between being goal-orientated and planning for your survival in the wilderness.

The stars came out in patches where the clouds had left space. I dozed until 2:00 a.m. and then thought about a lot of things, mainly Ro's forthcoming trip to Nepal and how long she'd be gone. There would be some suffering along the way – not being able to thrash things out as is our custom – to straighten out the kinks of everyday life. She'd come home changed. What kind of impact would this make on her life? And mine?

Nepal was such a different place. So unlike America. But she wanted to live with the poor. Well, she was going to do just that. What about getting sick? All the kids did – intestinal stuff – worms, parasites – all those things that plague you for the rest of your life. I must remember to ask our herbalist for a tincture to protect her; to ask our doctor for a homeopathic (a natural, non-toxic remedy) for those immunization shots she had to take; to give her chlorine drops for her drinking water. I must remember nothing. She had it all together, more so than I did. My mind ran on. Why do I worry so? Because a mother does. After all, like Ro says, what's a mother for? She'll be okay. She knows what to do. She's been preparing for a year now. Maybe I should start to prepare myself. The time is getting close and soon she'll be gone. Six months. I'll have to pull myself together and be brave and go on with my life. I've done it before. I'll do it again. I must.

Day 5: Closing the loop today, walking back to Eklund Lake where we had turned north to the high country a few days ago. A few days ago? More like a millennium. The sky was cloudy and it seemed warmer than usual. Had it been sunny we would have stayed and played awhile. Susan was still strange and I asked if anything was wrong. She felt the trip to be too much. She's used to resting every other day. Perhaps she should have told us before starting. She knew the itinerary. I wondered if she could forget this and go on or whether her apathy was going to cause a rift between us, ruining our remaining days.

We had come to an impasse, both mentally and physically: Pole Creek. Another wet crossing, except this one was deeper and wider than yesterday's. Again Ro took Susan's pack after dropping hers on the other side and together they got across with me close behind. While hiking through marsh and woods, passing a lot of lakes, Sue remained distant. I don't spend much time with anybody other than Marty and Roanne and when something is amiss, we talk about it. Even if it's difficult, the three of us know that bringing it into the open is the only way to clear the air – unless one wants to hang on to it because it answers some need – like shifting the blame onto somebody else for our problems, denying the guilt of not having researched the trip to see if it was doable, taking no responsibility.

Stopped for lunch on a fallen log and made some attempt at conversation. I felt I was absorbing her negativity at the same time that I was really enjoying myself. I decided to do something positive for myself so I "grounded" and sent Sue back her energy. I repeated it again and again and finally felt a little lighter. I needed to talk with Roanne. That would make me feel better.

Eventually Eklund Lake and a wonderful, flat, well-established campsite, the last one of the trip, appeared. It started to drizzle and the tent went up in a flash. The rain stopped. Susan wanted to rest. Roanne and I walked around the lake to the other side. She had found a knotted piece of fishing line on the trail and wanted to fish and I needed to be with her. While she looked for a long, straight stick, I untangled the line. With some rice cake crumbs for bait and a safety pin for a hook, I watched her climb to the end of a rock and toss in her line. She got a bite. That's what a positive attitude gets you. She finds pleasure in most things and as she said, she really didn't care if she caught anything – it was fun. The wind had picked up but she was determined. So I left her on the rock and went to filter water.

I saw Susan on the other side of the lake and waved. We all needed time alone. Six days living in close quarters can get old. Driven back by dark clouds that suddenly swept across the sky along with gusty winds and a few drops of rain, dinner was prepared in a dry, warm tent under a drizzle that softened the silence. Ramen, couscous, mashed potatoes and gravy – talk about carbohydrates. Wanting to finish all our food and keep only enough for tomorrow's final breakfast and lunch was our goal. Roanne and I walked up to the forks, sat on a rock and talked about our dilemma: Susan's attitude.

A mistake had been made but it was the ranger who had led us astray. Had I known it was twelve miles to Cook Lakes, I probably would not have suggested it. Sue's silence was a case of misplaced anger. So Ro and I complained, moaned and groaned and got it all out until our feelings cleared. The pressure was off. My heart sang once again while walking back to the tent, arm in arm, deciding to pull out the food bag and see what was left to eat. I asked Susan how she felt. She said she was glad to be getting out tomorrow. I was excited too but sad at the same time. Ro could have stayed forever.

Susan dropped off to sleep and Roanne and I played our last four games of gin rummy. She couldn't stay awake for another. A few welcome drops of rain and then stillness. As I lay listening for the rain and wild animals that might be lurking in the bushes, I thought about not having brought my journal. No sooner than that, the phrases started tumbling through my mind. Oh, for a paper and pen! I went over the miles and wrote about it in my mind. I went over the moments, desperately trying to memorize the emotion. I "grounded" between 3:00 a.m. and 5:00 a.m. and ran through the days again, concentrating on remembering.

Day 6: Roanne and I got up together and went to our respective spots in the bushes. Cloudy and cold. The dejection of the day before had disappeared. Going home. Mixed feelings of not wanting to leave the wilderness and wanting to end the trip and be alone together. Walking for so many years with just each other, it's difficult to have somebody else along.

My emotions stirred as the lake was left behind and I was glad to be last in line, alone with my thoughts and teary eyes. With every step forward I felt another in the opposite direction. Something was holding me back from leaving this mountain haven, a heaven on earth. Perhaps I realized I would have to wait a year to return.

Walking briskly because of the cold it didn't take long to reach Photographers Point. A déjà vu. Had it all happened? The picture of us missed before was taken and lunch was over-looked. The sun came out and a layer of clothing was shed. The trail was dry and the walk through familiar territory, easy.

I thought of the half-eaten peach left in the van. There are bears in the campground and it is said that they break into cars if they smell food. I got paranoid and envisioned the van with windows broken, sides smashed and insides torn out. Being so far from town, what would we do? Well, what I could do was forget about it, keep walking and enjoy the last few hours. Since you create your own reality, I might unconsciously make it happen.

The van was in the same condition as before except for some mice droppings around the half-eaten peach. We packed up, bought a loaf of bread at the local grocery and made some sandwiches while heading for Jackson, dreaming of a cool, crisp, green salad and hot shower.

It is always exciting to return to the known after spending so much time prowling around the unknown; being at the mercy of the weather, the wilderness, making life-threatening decisions in precarious situations whether to just go for it or let it go. It's good to be home.

A few days later I read a newspaper article about August 15-16, the night I experienced the unusual reflection of Heaven on Earth. This was the time of the Harmonic Convergence: a sort of momentary melody expected to be heard in the universe, a great shift in the earth's energy from warlike to peaceful, a five-year period of Earth's cleansing. Ancient legends about this particular Sunday and Monday were quite fascinating.

According to a prophecy handed down among the Hopi Indians living in northeast Arizona, August 17, 1987 was the date when "144,000 enlightened Sun Dance teachers would awaken the rest of humanity."

The Mayans, living in the Yucatan, marked August 16-17 as the climactic moment in a 5,000 year long process of global civilization, an evolutionary shift away from the global collective vision of competition and conflict towards collaboration.

The Aztecs, ancient Mexicans, believed in the prophecy given to them by one of the early incarnations of Quetzalcoatl, predicting a new period of heavens would dawn for the world on August 19, 1987. The start of a new world era!

It was remarkable to have been in the wilderness where it was so dark allowing the stars to shine so brightly. Something definitely had happened in the universe.

A month or so later we received a gift from Susan – a set of stainless steel camping pots just like hers.

The Bridger Teton Wilderness Headquarters responded to my complaint about the ranger by sending a map of the Winds and a rulebook. How governmentally typical.

VII

Cirque of the Towers

July 1988:

A year later in the middle of July, Roanne, just returned from her six-month Nepali adventure, and I picked Karen up at the airport and got ready to leave for the Wind Rivers the next morning. It took four-and-a-half hours to get to the Big Sandy Campground, thirty-five miles of it on a gravel/dirt, rutted road that rambled through a grand, unobstructed landscape where pronghorn antelope raced across faded green sagebrush plains. The parking area was crowded which shouldn't have surprised us since this entrance was the most popular in the southern part of the range. It was also the shortest route to the Cirque of the Towers, a renowned roost for rock climbers.

The first five miles of the trail followed the Big Sandy River to the lake of the same name. After lunch we climbed the steep switchbacks and traversed the slopes of Mitchell Peak for two miles to Jackass Pass on the Continental Divide. It was said that if a trail were designed to demoralize, it would be difficult to improve on this one. High on an arid, rocky ridge, above 11,000 feet where the air was thin, Karen got a throbbing headache. She hadn't acclimatized having come from sea level the day before.

Our first glimpse of Lonesome Lake, surrounded by the serrated crest of the Cirque, was a happy moment and we descended to a grassy valley, bushwhacking across a boulder field to find a campsite near a trickling brook. While sharing an orange, two bold marmots waddled over, insisting on staying after our efforts at shooing them away failed.

Over another boulder field to Hidden Lake, a tarn amidst profuse wildflowers, where Roanne swam in the frigid water while Karen and I watched, happy to be on our hindquarters. Back at our site our whole wheat rolls had been munched on by those cheeky rodents. Camp was set up and dinner devoured while the sun sank behind the Cirque leaving a rosy nimbus in a metallic blue-grey sky and Ro talked about Nepal. Karen wanted to hear her fascinating tale of living with a Nepali family in Kathmandu and a Gurung family in a tiny mountain village, Tang-Ting, close to Annapurna.

Ro and me in the Cirque

Day 2: After homemade granola while watching a bright sun climb into brilliant blue above Mitchell Peak, the three of us descended to the lake ringed with marsh marigolds, Lewis monkeyflowers, glacier lilies and alpine laurel. Two miles south along the North Popo Agie River, strenuous Lizard Head Trail climbed two thousand feet to the bare upper slopes of Windy Mountain. Above treeline on a wind-swept glacial plateau from where threatening thunderheads to the west could be seen, a lunch of smoked oysters, rolls, cheese and carrot sticks gave us time to rest among a peaceful panorama of peaks.

Valentine Lake

Cairns led us to the Bear's Ears Trail which descended a narrow alpine valley to Valentine Lake, over five miles. While putting up the tent, one of the poles snapped. We tried desperately to join the ends with a twig running through the center of the pole but the tension was too great. A crooked tent against a beautiful backdrop. Swimming in the icy water left us exhilarated and cleansed.

As I attempted to change the compressed gas cylinder to our camp stove, the can emptied into the air and all over us. There was only a little gas left when it was finally captured and I was lucky to have brought a few extras. Ramen, macaroni and cheese and tea warmed our insides while watching fish jump for flies. It was a quiet, warm, mellow evening and the day's problems faded as the wind riffled the water and the sky turned navy blue.

Day 3: A hazy orange sun hung in the sky as a late breakfast was enjoyed by the lake. Our once gracefully curved tent, now lopsided and awkward, had survived the night. The three of us, so alike in many ways, could exist together best in the back-country. It was as if the time apart didn't exist.

Grave Lake

11:00 a.m. Started down the long switchbacks toward the
South Fork of the Little Wind River, a rocky waterway that sliced
a perfect valley of wall-to-wall wildflowers, forested hillsides,
and a lone fisherman. Climbing steadily through limber pines to
crescent-shaped Grave Lake, a campsite materialized in a thick
grove as it started to drizzle and thunder rolled around the
peaks. The storm didn't last long and gave us time to stretch out
on a large flat rock by the lake, play in the shallow water and
explore the shoreline.

A full moon over Mt. Chauvenet glowed white in a hazy
sky. This desolate area had a strange stark beauty. Roanne fell
asleep early while Karen and I talked about feelings too difficult
to discuss over the phone in an attempt to soften the strain of our
relationship.

She spoke about her father, had thought she would have
been happy working for him, but there were a lot of issues with
his wife who couldn't handle her presence. There were some
awful scenes, now part of my daughter's life. They made me feel
helpless and guilty that I had allowed my first-born to be
involved in such a horrible situation.

LIKE A MIRROR UNFORSEEN A FULL MOON OVER GRAVE LAKE : R.D

Mt. Chauvenet

MT. CHAUVENETE
GRAVE LAKE
KAREN

I was having trouble with Karen and Maxine because of their decision to stay with their father when Roanne, Marty and I moved west. I was jealous of their relationship with him and tried hard to release my resentment in order not to injure my love for my daughters. Not being together for long absences made it difficult. There was so much animosity between my ex and myself and the girls had to find some balance in a difficult situation. Not an easy task. Somebody always gets hurt.

Startled by the sound of footsteps outside our tent, our conversation came to a sudden halt. Frozen in space, hearts pounding. It was silly to think that a thin piece of nylon between us and whatever was outside provided safety. Tried desperately to be quiet while searching for the firecrackers in Roanne's pack; as Karen held the tiny explosive I had a match ready to strike. A twig cracked. We waited expectantly but must have finally dozed because it was 3:00 a.m. when the sound was heard again. My nylon bag rustled as I changed position and two large ears went up in the screened triangular doorway of the tent. A deer. What a relief!

Day 4: Slightly overcast, good for crossing 11,890-foot Hailey Pass. After breakfast the three of us started out, shedding a layer of clothing while climbing around the sheer wall of 12,504-foot Mt. Hooker, the steepest of its height in the Winds. A couple had just come down from the pass and let us know we were going up the hard way. Starting the ascent in fine gravel and sand, hardly stable enough for a foothold, it got more vertical while the switchbacks shortened, becoming barely visible. Clutching at loose, rocky soil and crawling on all fours, the top was gained and a grand view of undulating peaks as far as the eye could see.

After a gradual descent to Twin Lakes and a stop for lunch, we climbed to Pyramid Lake where the trail ended. It didn't take long to find a campsite in the boulder-strewn tundra that rimmed the tiny lake. Setting up quickly to avoid a passing storm, its tailwind shaking the tent, the late afternoon was spent in a warm, luxurious tent, lazily braiding each other's hair, plucking eyebrows, stray whiskers, filing fingernails and grooming each other like chimpanzees. It was so normal being with Karen, especially in the mountains, but I was in total denial of what our lives were really about. I desperately wanted everything to be okay. It wasn't. A full moon lit the sky and once again, I was alone in a quiet corner of the cosmos.

East Fork Lakes – Valley of the Walls

Day 5: Up as the sun peered over Pyramid Peak and eating breakfast as it warmed the tent. While the girls climbed 11,172-foot Midsummer Dome, I sketched the East Fork Valley peaks, anxiously watching them on top, relieved when they reached bottom. I could tell that Roanne loved having Karen back in her

Midsummer Dome

life. She could do stuff with her that I wouldn't do, like hike to the top of the Dome. I remember how close they used to be when living in Vermont. Even though being together now was wonderful, there were unexpressed emotions that would have to be faced – one day.

Heading out, we hiked to the lakes below, bushwhacked over a heavily treed hillside and up a boulder-strewn creek to Mae's Lake. Reluctantly leaving this realm of peaks, divides, glaciers, basins and high plateaus, I felt compelled to keep looking back, for that indelible impression to be etched on my mind until the alpine reaches became available again. Instead of spending our last night at a lower altitude, a decision was made to hike the two and a half miles to Shadow Lake on the west side of the Cirque and stay above treeline.

There wasn't much choice for a site and our tent ended up too close to the lake. Some pasta dumped in the shallow water by an indifferent camper upset us. The sinking sun left a vermillion, purple, orange sky and its glow washed the rocks with warm red while the valley dropped into dusk and finally darkness. Tomorrow was our last day.

Day 6: It was an easy nine-mile walk out. The long dusty drive towards civilization had us concerned about running out of gas but luck was with us. Filled up in Boulder, bought a six-pack of Coronas in Pinedale, and Roanne drove home. A fresh green salad from the garden, pasta with pesto sauce, hot showers and some new tales to tell. It had been a good hike – 6 days, 40 miles – with no mishaps but a bent tent.

Karen left the next day. There were a lot of tears. My stomach clenched a few times – such strong emotion. That was to be our last trip together and the three of us seemed to grow farther apart the closer we tried to get. She called when she got home to tell me that she was having a tough time being back. I knew something was bothering her. After much prodding, she confided that her boyfriend had admitted to having cheated while she was away. Not a nice welcome home. A daughter's hell is a mother's heartache.

VIII

Fire in the Mountains

August 1988:
The summer started with reports of a drought scorching America's Midwest. In Jackson the heat of June had reached a then-all-time-high of 96 degrees. These record-breaking temperatures began to dry out forests that had already been subjected to two mild winters and on the hill behind our cabin some wells had gone dry. Fires began as expected but in July the magnitude of the fire season suddenly became apparent. The national media turned from the plight of the Midwestern farmers and converged on the Yellowstone ecosystem to report about the most volatile and political fire story in the country's history.

We were living in the small town of Kelly in Grand Teton National Park, ninety miles south of Yellowstone. The fire closest to us was contained and so on August 22, Roanne and I drove south towards Pinedale and the Elkhart Park entrance to the Wind Rivers. Because there was a plume of smoke on the way to the trailhead, a stop at the ranger station was called for. A fire at Fayette Lake was just a little blaze and nothing to worry about. However Knapsack Col, a steep gap on the divide between Peak Lake Valley and Titcomb Basin, an off-trail section of the Highline Trail, was devoid of snow, this being such a dry year, giving us a chance to cross the mountains, making a loop rather than retracing our steps.

The parking lot was full as usual but there weren't many people on the trail. After a nine-mile march to Seneca Lake, a descent of two miles to Lost Lake, lost in the woods, ringed by high rocky ridges, was tough on our knees. A site by a rushing creek away from the few tents provided some privacy. I was tired. After dinner and a walk in the woods to stretch our legs and see our surroundings, the two of us lay back in the tent and studied tomorrow's route while a full moon lit this small, secluded valley leaving us in semi-darkness.

At 2:00 a.m. I awoke with a burning sensation in the middle of my stomach. I remember experiencing the same feeling when Roanne had left for Nepal last year. I was terrified about her going so far away and for such a long time. Was I scared about climbing that high col? Anxious about the prospect of disappointing her? Heights bothered me. I changed sides, tried lying on my back to relieve the pressure and finally fell asleep.

Day 2: In the morning I discussed my predicament with my daughter. She didn't care what we did or how we got there, she was just happy to be in the wilderness again. I felt better. The pressure was off and the pain almost gone. But the smoke seen yesterday had spread over the ridge to fill the draw at the south end of the lake. A wrangler on horseback crossed the stream to ask about the fire, wondering if he should take his group out the way we had come in. I was just as concerned heading into the mountains for three more days. After telling him our plans, he said the fire could be seen from the high country and that would tell us what to do. He drew a map in the dirt showing us a more northerly exit in case the fire should continue to spread.

Ro and I packed up and climbed to Fremont Crossing, uneasy about going on. Two hikers passed wondering if their car back at Elkhart Park might have melted. Crossing Shannon Pass the smoke whorl could be seen in the distance.

The trail into Peak Lake Valley, a rocky quadrangle of lakes and huge boulders, was steep and stony, and the creek carrying the meltwaters of Stroud Glacier above became the headwaters of the famous Green River. Hiking around this opaque turquoise tarn, a campsite emerged and dinner was prepared. Exhausted, I tested myself using kinesiology taught to me by our naturopath, and found that I was full of acid rain (rainfall made acidic by atmospheric pollution, the main cause being the industrial burning of coal and other fossil fuels, causing environmental harm to forests and lakes). That could have been the cause of my discomfort the previous night. A few minutes after taking our homeopathic pills I felt better. (Homeopathy is a system of alternative medicine that is based on the law of similars which states that a remedy can cure a disease if it produces in a healthy person symptoms to those of the disease.)

After washing the dust off in the lake, a walk up the canyon towards the col relieved my apprehension. It looked steep as our necks arched back trying to pick a path. I was feeling positive about the climb and Roanne reassured me that our plan could be abandoned if I felt threatened. The sun went down behind the rocky outcrops and the valley deepened in color. I slept well.

Day 3: Up before the sun and walking soon after. Reaching the "trail's end" sign was a bit unnerving. The col came into view, so high ahead of us, but disappeared while walking along a creek that went underground although its gurgle could still be heard. A few cairns here and there.

The slow, long climb began. The route got steeper and rougher with no indication of any sort of trail markings. Usually you can pick out a boot impression or a bit of a worn path. Not here. Approaching what seemed to be the top, a faint trail appeared and as I scrambled up the last few feet, Roanne turned and reached for me. I didn't need help, exhilarated at being where I was, 12,240 feet in the air. Knapsack Col – the saddle between Twins and Winnifred Peaks with Peak Lake Valley on the west, Titcomb Basin, one of our favorites, on the east and the upper end of the Twins Glacier at our feet.

The basin below was formed by one of the range's highest and steepest escarpments – the west faces of Mt. Helen, Mt. Sacajewea and Fremont Peak – all over 13,000 feet. Three narrow alpine lakes dropped from Dinwoody Pass, first steeply and then gradually, to 10,346-foot Island Lake, our destination. Creeping along the glacier's edge, an area appeared that looked safe and, holding hands, I slid into Roanne's footsteps while the melting snow rushed far beneath us. A relentless sun had softened the snowpack between the crevices and I knew we were on unstable ground. Suddenly she, now ahead, disappeared between two huge boulders. A paralyzing chill went through me until I heard her shout that she was okay.

It was a long way down. Struggling to keep on top of the snow while glissading to the valley floor was demanding. Muddy ground was never so welcome as we finally touched bottom and pulled off our boots and socks to wade in the cold, clear water of the upper lake. Cooled by a soft breeze, a leisurely lunch was relished. With our boots tied to our packs, a change to flip-flops was welcomed for a walk along the lakeshore to the entrance of the basin where the two of us reluctantly passed through the rocky portal leaving Shangri-la behind.

Three miles to Island Lake and our tent went up in the same spot it did the last time. The water was cool on our burnt, dusty skin and after washing shirts and socks, a large dinner was cooked in the tent. The temperature dropped as a stroll to the sandy beach at the far end of the lake found us sitting in the first row watching the sun drop off the end of our world.

Day 4: I awoke abruptly at 5:00 a.m. and could barely make out the faint outline of Roanne next to me. Peering outside, I tried desperately to distinguish something. Alarmed at the lack of visibility and the smell of smoke, I woke her. "We've got to get out," I said, as she sleepily tried to focus on me. A large nebulous orange globe was rising over Elephant Head and the air, filled with smoke, created a bizarre, unearthly landscape. We packed in a flash and, barely able to breathe, wet our bandannas, stretched them across our faces and started the fifteen-mile hike out.

It was eerie walking with no identifying markers. The mountains and lakes couldn't be seen, just a few feet of trail before us. Two backpackers suddenly emerged from the fog, their faces covered. They had walked in from Elkhart Park and were deciding whether to continue or turn back. They didn't know anything more about the fire.

The worst of the smoke was left behind at Seneca Lake but suddenly Roanne couldn't continue. She slid her backpack to the ground and collapsed on a rock. I checked her out with our homeopathics and found her full of acid rain. Minutes after taking the "acid rain" pills, she was ready to go on.

Our tiny homeopathic pills had rescued us time and again. Roanne returned from Nepal with a staph infection. I picked it up and tried everything to get rid of it, everything alternative that is. My naturopath sent me some homeopathics. After one month with no success, Marty and I took a trip to St. Anthony, Idaho, just across the mountains. Dr. Long, our long-time naturopath, took a swab of the infection, made a homeopathic remedy and one and a half days later the sore dried up. Quite amazing! That was just one of the many times with such success.

The van hadn't melted, the parking lot was considerably less crowded, and a cold beer quenched my parched throat while Roanne drove back to Jackson Hole, the Yellowstone fires and Marty.

"On all continents, saints have struggled to free their souls from a world tainted figuratively by evil, a real world of plagues and boils and starvation that make the promise of another world, beyond death, sweet.

"Yet their world was clean by comparison. Smoke was smoke, rain was not a witch's brew, and the earth grew hemlock and nightshade and cobra, poisons which were old and could be learned.

"This is a different world, soft, deadly, altered beyond recall, and we must live in it and try not to kill each other. We must bear unprecedented threat, the anger that rises from fear, and the loss that yawns beneath our streets.

"The wilderness is good, but it is only a respite. Only the self-deluding could find Eden up here, knowing what we know. But this is my heart's country."

C.L. Rawlins

IX

New Fork Lakes

In 1989, Marty and I found eighty acres of land on the Blaeberry River, outside Golden, British Columbia, Canada. In the next few years we built a tarpaper shack, as some of the neighbors called it, and traveled between Golden and Jackson Hole.

August 1990:
On the 20th of August, with five days off work, Roanne and I left for a walk in the Winds. Her Volkswagen bug smelled of gas after filling up in Jackson which caused some concern on the drive south towards the Cora turnoff and the seventeen miles on gravel to the New Fork Lakes entrance. While taking a last look at her car to make sure nothing important was left behind, a pack trip on horseback was leaving and the wrangler told us about "one of the best campsites" in the canyon.

From the Narrows Campground the trail climbed steadily through a grove of aspens, stayed high on a sage-covered slope above Upper New Fork Lake, and dropped to a sandy beach, a favorite picnic place of ours. It finally crossed the forest boundary into wilderness at 3.4 miles. Roanne and I climbed into the steep, rock-walled New Fork Canyon and after 6.7 miles and two tricky river crossings, the two of us ascended to a meadow, exhausted and desperate for a site. Fording the river again to a well-used area with a lot of horse manure, probably the spot that the wrangler had mentioned, the tent was pitched under a tree and dinner prepared just as it started to drizzle. After hanging our food a good distance from the tent, it had to be lowered to add our toothpaste and then once more for a used teabag.

Not having spent much time together in the last four months she and I felt disoriented which was evident by having to hang our food three times. Marty and I had been building our cabin in the Canadian wilderness while Roanne was thinking about college again in Olympia, Washington. It rained softly while sudden wind gusts shook the tent, thunder rumbled in the distance and lightning reflected overhead.

Day 2: At 7:00 a.m. the rainfly was wet, the ground, soaked and the sky, blue. High ridges reflected the rising sun while the valley floor was still in shade. Treetops turned gold while hiking the two miles to the steep, narrow Palmer Canyon Trail – a rough climb with full packs, thirty-five to forty pounds. It was cold and windy at Palmer Lake and we didn't linger over lunch. The Double-top Mountain Trail headed east for six miles to Summit Lake, passing through basins, dells and gulches, losing and gaining altitude continuously. Suddenly, cresting a rise, an open meadow with No Name Lakes came into view. Around a sprawling hillock, isolated, cerulean Summit Lake, cradled in extensive tundra-like meadows materialized against an azure sky pierced by the peaks of the Continental Divide. The country fell away on all sides and clouds drifted at eye level.

tent

Tent at Summit Lake

The 10,500-foot terrace on the west side of the Winds was a country of clustered pine and spruce scattered through expansive meadows of wild flowers, meandering streams, and countless lakes, ponds and marshes. One could walk for miles without losing altitude. Quinoa and vegetables at 7:00 p.m. and two hands of gin rummy sent us to bed, too tired to talk.

Day 3: 8:00 a.m. Awoke to a blue sky. After yesterday's strenuous hike, relaxing was our aim for the day. Roamed around the lake, and tried, without success, to talk a fisherman out of one of his trout. After a superb dinner of pasta, vegetables and a salad of freshly picked mertensia (bluebell) leaves, our garbage was burned and the fire kept going while the temperature dropped. Roanne wanted me to try her new down sleeping bag that I had sewn from a Frostline kit. It felt like I was cradled in a cloud, convincing me to make one for myself and another for Marty. After getting into my twenty-year old bag, she remarked, "God, Ma, this is what the Boy Scouts get by on."

Day 4: At 8:30 a.m. there were light clouds floating in a basin of blue. After breakfast I packed my smaller backpack with rain gear, lunch, warm clothes, map, first aid kit, water, and along with Ro, headed north through Green River Pass to the Glacier Trail cutoff, a poorly marked junction that was difficult to find. We climbed to Vista Pass, descended to the Canyon of the Green and made our way one thousand feet up through rockslides to Cube Rock Pass. Aqua-blue Peak Lake, a hole in the rocks, came into view far below. Up a steep, rocky path to 11,150-foot Shannon Pass and on to dramatic Elbow Lake, nestled in a barren basin of smooth rock. Hail forced us to seek cover under Roanne's poncho and, quickly dressing in all our clothes, lunch was devoured while leaning against a boulder shielded from a sharp wind. Some ginseng tincture warmed us as diced hailstones bounced off the poncho and the ground around us. When the sun appeared we continued on through craggy, fault-fractured country so beautiful, a promise was made to return.

After a long stormy day, the depression of Summit Lake in the distance brought a feeling of relief. A dark wall of cloud was moving in and the wind had picked up with sounds of thunder on its tail.

I was getting my long hair brushed while enjoying some dried bananas and tea. There always came a time when the gas cylinder had to be changed and the thought came up about buying a stove that required a fuel bottle with fuel for refilling, not adding to the world's waste.

A welcome dinner fulfilled us while talking about the men in our lives and what they had in common. Her father was mirrored in her choices and if I had trouble with him, why wouldn't she? A storm suddenly descended upon us, shaking our shelter and causing the rainfly to balloon and beat against the tent. Our discussion picked up after the outside became less of an issue and continued until Roanne fell asleep. She woke at 1:30 a.m. to answer the call of nature and our talk resumed until 4:00 a.m.

Our life choices segued into our perpetual conversation on the wilderness. Why was wilderness so essential to our lives? "I love a primitive life with no amenities," Roanne said. "The mountains force you into it. I love hot baths but love to bathe in cold water, to carry everything on my back and rely on nobody. It has taught me to trust myself. There are no mirrors, no peer pressure. I don't like the familiarity of social life where everyone is polite, putting up façades. In the mountains all that is dropped. I just like being in the wind, the trees, amidst the rocks. That's where I feel most natural. Being with you, you're just the closest to nature and I can spill my heart out. There's nothing to judge, nothing gets in the way. Time is very different here, something felt and lived. Actually there's no time – just morning, day and night. Being so damaged by the divorce, the mountains are soothing, a visceral cushion. That's why I go with you."

I couldn't have put it better myself. A mother needs time, with no distractions, to tell her daughter about her own life. There is nobody else but me for her out here. She's got me cornered and can ask whatever she pleases. I wish my mother had told me more about her life. I knew very little and didn't know then that I would have liked to know more. She was a complex woman with a lot of secrets. My father intimated certain things about her but never got into anything in depth, nor did I ask. When I did bring up sensitive family issues like my adoption, my inquisitiveness was discouraged. Nobody wanted to talk about anything.

Day 5: By dawn the storm had passed. Rather than hiking the Highline to the New Fork Trail that crossed a divide to Lozier Lakes and our next campsite, a decision was made on a diagonal route (no trail). Apprehensive without a compass or topographic map, a new way out rather than retracing our steps was tempting.

Heading west on the Doubletop Mountain Trail we passed No Name Lakes and searched the landscape for cairns. Finis Mitchell, the American forester based in Wyoming, described this route: "As long as Glover Peak, the highest summit west of the Highline Trail, was to the northeast, keep going around it."

With eyes on Glover, Ro and I headed north, passing lakes and tarns and climbing ridges that approached like ocean waves. Thunderheads in the distance roused my concern and figuring them to arrive by late afternoon, I hoped to be off this high plateau. Being above timberline we could see for miles except what was over the next ridge.

The sight of a footprint in the gravelly earth helped allay our burgeoning fear. Roanne finally dropped her pack and ran ahead to see beyond the next ridge while I rested on a rock. Another ridge. I was getting worried; if near the cliffs, then we were too far west. It was the third time when I heard a yell. She could see the trail far below.

Finally finding a break in the escarpment Roanne climbed down while I lowered my pack over the edge into her waiting arms. As the slope became more gradual, a creek surfaced and, following it to the New Fork Trail, I humbly got down on my hands and knees and kissed the earth.

It was late afternoon when Lozier Lakes appeared. The storm front was moving in quickly. There was no level ground and we hastily set up the tent in a tiny area fringed with stunted spruce, cooked dinner and climbed into our bags with not a moment to spare. The tempest descended in all its fury. Thunder shook my insides and lightning flashed relentlessly. I had left our stainless steel pots at the doorway and reached out to push them as far away as possible for fear a lightning bolt might be lured our way. The rumbling rolled in from the distance, gaining momentum as it passed overhead and pressed on. The lightning crackled, warning of another blast and I waited, preparing myself. On and on into the night, hour after hour, the turbulence even woke Roanne who usually slept through everything. Not all high mountain storms get me this worried.

As the hours passed the storm moved eastward, making room for its aftermath – driving rain, more lightning and wind.

Day 6: At first light I peeked out into the silence to find us buried under a heavy layer of snow. A decision to pack up during a lull and head down where we would be less of a target was made. The sun peered out periodically, warming our chilled bodies and melting our frosty hiking boots while descending into the trees under a light snow. Our footsteps were muffled in the hush of falling flakes and the stillness sensitized our awareness and slowed our mindless hurry home.

Switchbacking two-and-a-half miles down a steep canyon amongst lodgepole pine, subalpine fir and Engelmann spruce, Ro and I traveled dreamlike through a soft veil of crystalline mist, hardly speaking, enclosed in our thoughts. Dropping towards the river, the forest changed to stands of quaking aspen, Oregon grape, yarrow, aster and lupine. Finally the two of us reached the canyon floor, passed through New Fork Park, our first campsite a century ago, and as the day cleared, emerged from the trees to view the lakes in the far distance.

Our wet boots and soggy sweatpants made the fifteen-mile walk out uncomfortable. At the car, a handshake, congratulating each other on the completion of yet another walk in the wilderness and safe return from a heroic hike. Next time the compass would go into our packs first.

As always, I had mixed emotions upon leaving. The time with Roanne was very precious and, as our ties were renewed, our similarities reminded me that I had blood relatives on this earth. Being adopted without knowing my history, I often forgot that. Able to be silent with a full understanding of our feelings made me aware of our secure connection and love in a world fraught with alienation and suffering. These walks were our private time to lower the dam and deal with emotions held in check when apart. The feeling of survival gave me an independence and strength that I could live by my own wits. We drove back to Kelly with a deep calmness, satisfied at having taken the time to replenish our mother-daughter bond once again.

X

Lake O'Hara

1991:

During the summer Marty's estranged daughter suddenly planned to visit him in Jackson Hole with a friend. They hadn't seen one another for years, and since Roanne and I didn't want to be around, we left for Golden for a few weeks of hiking in the Canadian Rockies. She might have found it difficult sharing Marty and he would be more relaxed being alone.

The cabin was as it was left except for some mice droppings. In the ten pounds of mail that had accumulated since our last trip, there was a circular for Festival '91 in Nelson, British Columbia featuring Joan Baez. The concert was three days away.

It had been cloudy. Rain might be a problem so our ponchos were packed along with food and camping gear for an overnight. Saturday morning saw us on our way for the six-hour drive to this small, historic "nuclear-free" town on the southern tip of Kootenay Lake. After stocking up on groceries at the co-op, Roanne treated me to the concert tickets, and then drove to the backcountry cutoff, ignoring the warning about grizzlies in the glacier area. The sixteen, extremely difficult kilometers up the winding, rocky canyon took over an hour. After gathering wood for our tiny stove in the back of the pickup, a dinner of corn tortillas, tofu slices, salsa, diced onions and a large salad was enjoyed. The stove took the chill off the night air and both of us feel asleep to the sound of rushing water and rain on the roof.

It was still raining in the early hours of the morning. I wondered if it would clear in time for the outdoor concert and worried about the condition of the road back to the highway below. Suddenly the rain stopped and a hike before breakfast sounded invigorating. A sign warned of a bear corridor through which the trail passed reminding us to make noise; easy switchbacks for a mile and a half to impassable snow. An attempt to walk around the lake was interrupted because of heavy snow as well.

The fairgrounds on the banks of Kootenay Lake just outside Nelson were bustling; blankets, tarps, plastic squares and sleeping bags circled the foreground. Ro and I rushed back to the truck to gather our stuff and were lucky to find a grassy rectangle about fifteen feet in front of center stage. After stretching out our ponchos and securing the corners with rocks, the two of us dropped onto the center of our site to guard it for the next ten hours. Talk about territorial rights.

At 3:00 p.m. huge clouds collected around the Selkirk Peaks while the grounds were filling up. By 4:00 p.m. there were patches of blue in the sky. Roanne investigated the other band-stands while I stood guard and then switched, giving us both a chance to look around.

It was finally 5:00 p.m., food was everywhere and blankets extended beyond the rear bank of lights and speakers. At 7:30 p.m. the first performer, Sarah McLachlan, then an unknown singer, appeared. She was loud and attendants handed out earplugs to the few rows up front; a Brazilian band followed. The stage was finally cleared, instruments hauled off, floor swept and without warning, Joan was there, in jeans, sneakers, white turtleneck and black jacket. A few words to the controller, a glance at her accompanist, and she reached for her guitar. I can't remember her opening set because I was in shock. Gracias a la Vida, Diamonds and Rust, Amazing Grace – did we remember Woodstock a hundred-and-fifty years ago? – Forever Young, The Night They Drove Old Dixie Down, Railroad Boy, Gabe's Song; a few wonderful warm words to her dedicated fans about her politics and how different they were from Bob Hope's who had performed the night before, and she was gone, all five-and-a-half feet of her. She reappeared for one encore amidst shouts and clapping and the glorious evening was over.

After returning to the truck with our two torn tickets, the headlights wouldn't turn on. The fuses were fine but the wire hung limply from one of the battery terminals. It was difficult to handle earthly things after such an event, but the connection was made and a drive to a small campground on the outskirts of town, managed. It was midnight and having just witnessed a phenomenon, the two of us were too wired to sleep.

In the morning heading north through the Slocan Valley, a stop in Nakusp for a quick swim at the beach and the purchase of some fresh lychees, vegetables and grapes was made, enough to keep us at the cabin for a few days. Talked all the way home about what Roanne wanted to do with her life. She was unsure whether to stay in Canada or move back to the States. However there were more important things to do right now, like hiking in the Canadian Rockies which neither of us had ever done.

After pouring over our maps, Lake O'Hara in Banff National Park was our choice. I had heard it was one of the most beautiful areas with twenty-five lakes and some of the highest and most rugged mountains in the entire range.

Day 1: Early the next morning a drive through Yoho National Park got us to the Banff trailhead. About ten minutes in I froze and called to Roanne, just ahead of me. A black bear and two cubs blocked our path. Transfixed, we watched as she whisked her babies up a tree and trundled off to settle behind a large dead tree trunk. Growling softly, she shifted her weight, snorted at her cubs bouncing in the upper branches, warning them of the danger at hand, and they, playfully and unconcerned, went on with their ruckus.

Carefully watching her out of the corners of my eyes so as not to be threatening, I whispered to Roanne to start walking. Advancing slowly, trying not to make any quick moves, the two of us finally passed her and rounded a bend, looking back every few seconds to make sure she wasn't following. That was a close call. I don't like surprising a bear, especially a sow and cubs. With all my professed fear of bears, I was the one who got us through that time as Roanne reminded me.

Continuing through a lush forest of lodgepole pine, almost never losing the sound of Cataract Creek on our left, Narao

Lakes were passed along with a quick glimpse of the O'Hara fire road; up some switchbacks and finally a view of Mt. Victoria and the Watchtower; over a few rockfalls to a four-way junction where the trail crossed Morning Glory Creek and, at the next fork, turned east for two miles to the campground.

There's a bus that rides the restricted Lake O'Hara Fire Road taking visitors to this sensitive alpine area in summertime. To maintain a wilderness experience, Parks Canada uses a quota system to limit the number of visitors using the public bus service thereby controlling access to the valley.

It was close to 4:00 p.m. when our packs were dropped at a small, groomed site beneath spruce trees and the tent set up on a rectangular, packed-gravel platform that looked like a raised garden bed. The campground had two kitchen shelters which provided a place to cook meals and dry out wet gear. There were wood stoves, one fire pit, grey water disposal, outhouses, firewood with splitting maul, and treated well water (not always available early and late season). Ro and I walked down to the communal area for water and stored our food and backpacks in the animal-proof shelter, a small building with a heavy metal door that was divided inside by a solid wall for garbage on the right. This was a grizzly corridor and cleanliness was of utmost importance. A warning not to allow any rinse water to fall on the rocks under the tap because odors accumulated was posted. All this was new to us. Since hiking together the two of us have always been on our own, bears or no bears. Here we were forced to hang out with humans. It was comforting, for the first time, not to be alone.

A mile to the secluded Lake O'Hara Lodge, a square-log, Swiss-chalet type structure built in 1926 by the Canadian Pacific Railway – 11 km, (almost 7 miles) from the nearest road and completely off-grid, situated on beautiful Lake O'Hara, a true alpine wilderness paradise. Upon entering, the manager instructed us to take off our boots and leave them by the door. The walls around the comfortable living room with large stone fireplace were lined with art – warm and inviting. There was a photography exhibit in progress but afternoon tea had already been served. Guests were milling about, nicely dressed and very proper, unlike us in our grungy hiking clothes. That's why the receptionist looked at us like she did. I'm surprised she didn't ask us to leave.

Dinner in the kitchen shelter was different and it wasn't long before we turned in for the night which passed peacefully.

Day 2: Lake Oesa, our destination, was set in a high, desolate cirque on the backside of Lake Louise. The two of us made our way along the shoreline trail to the end of the lake, climbed the steep switchbacks to the top of a cliff, continued over talus and scree slopes, through stunted forest, and up a succession of steep, rocky outcrops on stone steps carved by Lawrence Grassi*. Across fragile meadows enclosed by high cliffs found us climbing to the top of a grassy slope, through a rock gulley to the lake surrounded by high rock walls, frozen most of the year; walked around the lake for a glimpse of Abbot's Pass, the major alpine route between Lakes O'Hara and Louise, and the stone hut at the top of the steep couloir. The climb must be easier on the other side because nothing in the world would get me up this one.

I was afraid to take any of the alpine routes which is what this valley is known for; the guidebook states, "there are five alpine routes above the O'Hara basin for experienced hikers comfortable with route finding, heights and traversing exposed terrain. Many of the routes are extremely exposed to the elements and to elevation. A fall could be deadly." Of one of the trails, it says "The acrophobic should avoid this trail."

So, in the afternoon we crossed to the other side of the valley, through an alpine meadow dotted with brilliant wild-flowers, past the Elizabeth Parker Hut (maintained by the Alpine

*A note about Lawrence Grassi: After he retired from the Canmore coal mines, Grassi spent several summers in the Lake O'Hara area where he worked as a park warden. Although he loved to climb, he also loved to build trails in the mountains. His beautiful rockwork has been used by generations of hikers to reach the high valleys of Lake Oesa and Lake McArthur.

Club of Canada) towards Schäffer Lake, a glacial lake with Mt. Biddle as a backdrop en route to McArthur Lake. The trail proceeded through stands of larch (although larches are conifers, they are deciduous trees that lose their leaves in the autumn) that followed the edge of the cliffs and, after leaving the forest, branched into two circuits – the high and low level circuits. I got stuck on a steep, narrow ledge where a stone stairway carved into a cleft in the rock started up a precipitous slope and had to turn back. It didn't bother Roanne but two women behind us followed suit. Spent the rest of a hot afternoon in the meadows cooled by a silent breeze.

That night an idea came to us about hiking out in the morning, buying some food at the store in Field, a tiny town on the Trans-Canada Highway which passes through the middle of Yoho National Park, and crossing into the Yoho Valley for a few more days of hiking.

Day 3: 10:00 a.m., a stroll to the lodge and a call to the grocery store in Field to find out when they closed made our decision easy. After an endless, forced, eight-mile march, watching cautiously around every bend for bear, Roanne drove to the store, arriving minutes before closing, she and I bought what our diet could endure, then started the fourteen-mile road to Yoho, the eighth wonder of the world with its compressed, stacked switchbacks where buses had to backup to negotiate the turns. In a parking area below the 820-foot Takakkaw Falls, second highest waterfall in Canada, dinner was welcomed and sleep overtook us while listening to thundering water – lucky that no rangers came by because we didn't have a permit to camp there.

Day 4: Heading into Yoho Valley the next morning, passing numerous waterfalls for which this valley is known – Point Lace Falls, Angels Staircase, Laughing Falls – the moderate trail brought us to a high bank overlooking the upper reaches of the Yoho River where the glacier had receded far back into the canyon; lunched on the rocky slope while talking about the differences of hiking in Canada as opposed to the U.S. – fewer people, an older, more culturally diverse crowd, increased restrictions and lower altitudes. The sun felt good while staring at the empty canyon once filled with ice. The greenhouse effect the government had denied for years was no doubt having an effect, shrinking the glaciers and drying up the land.

Retracing our steps to the junction, a mile back, the two of us started the relentless ascent to the chalet at the base of the very impressive 260-foot Twin Falls, two massive waterfalls plunging to the valley floor. A couple was nice enough to offer us a few dollars for a pot of tea to accompany our cookies while basking in the hot sun on the porch of the Twin Falls Tea House, a two-story rustic log building that could accommodate five people. Roanne was so impressed by the place that she applied for a job for the next summer. You had to trek in with supplies a few times a week, do a lot of menial chores, and live in the glorious backcountry of Yoho National Park.

Continuing on, rather than backtracking, Ro and I made our way across a broad boulder field, descended into the depths of this valley of miniature clay terraces and crusty rocks, passed Marpole Lake and met up with the little Yoho Valley Trail (adding another three miles to our day). After getting some money from our truck, a walk back to the campground to pay the couple who were genuinely surprised to see us, was just barely managed. That added another one-and-a-half-miles to a thirteen-and-a-half-mile hike.

From Field I called Marty to let him know that all was well, the two of us were out of the mountains having walked ourselves ragged, and ready to head back to Jackson Hole.

Twin Falls, Marty's Sketch

XI

Scab Creek

September 1992:
It had been overcast for days and too late in the season to
postpone our trip into the Winds. This was a new area for us,
Scab Creek, the second lowest entrance in the range and one of
the most strenuous. The sun was shining when we stopped in
Pinedale for a trowel and two pounds of Jonathan apples, the
first of the season.

It was cool at 11:30 a.m. when Roanne and I started up the
steep hillside and continued to climb the three laborious miles to
Toboggan Lakes. At Little Divide Lake under a few clouds, lunch
on a log, our legs dangling weightlessly. Past Lightning Lakes
summer changed to fall and sweat pants replaced our shorts. I
have never hiked the Winds in June or September when there
wasn't snow.

Just beyond the lakes the mountains came into view and
finally the south fork of Boulder Creek where a rough wooden
sign pointed to Dream Lake, our destination. It had been a long
day and I understood why this was not a popular trail.

Roanne found a spot and our tent went up before the first
raindrops. After dinner and washing our dishes by the creek
below, twigs were collected for a fire while picking our way back
to the tent in the dark. It was too beautiful to sleep and a fire
kept us warm while sitting on a rock staring at the peaks. Far
across the lake the flicker of another flame could be seen through
the trees. At about 10:00 p.m. the wind picked up and it turned
cold. After smothering the fire we climbed into our down bags
and watched the embers glow through the tent opening. While
talking, I could hear Roanne's even breathing and realized she

had fallen asleep. At these times I could see her as a little girl
with no cares in the world, no bears in her thoughts, no sisters
on her mind. Warm, quiet, comfortable and still – just as I liked it
to be.

Our tent at Dream Lake overlooking the lake

Day 2: It was light at 7:00 a.m. The sky was blue and clouds
hung around the peaks. No stiff muscles. Amazing! Ro and I
explored the Dream Lake environs, walked south towards the
Bonneville Basin, but deciding a whole day was needed to do it
justice, returned to the tent for lunch. With our down jackets and
books, a narrow sandy beach passed on our morning stroll
beckoned us. A few hours were spent reading while a beaver
floated lazily to and fro. Suddenly a distant sound disturbed the
silence. This was sheep-grazing country and there they came,
swarming over the far slope with two cowboys alongside.

The soporific sound of sheep droned in the distance while
macaroni and cheese warmed our insides under an azure sky
with a few cloud shadows crossing distant peaks, dissolving and
leaving clear blue. After building a fire, the only way to stay out

in the cold, she and I watched the firmament fill with starry galaxies. During the night a hooting owl came closer until it sounded as if it were next to the tent and then receded gradually into the distance.

Day 3: The day began with too much oatmeal which was eaten anyway. While washing our dishes at the creek, Sybil from Salt Lake wandered by looking for the trail sign. She had been in the northern Winds for eight weeks and had left her partner two days ago with their tent and most of their food. It was because of his temper, she said. Happy to meet some women on the trail because the men she encountered wanted only to pamper her and treat her like a woman. Wanting to hitch a ride to Salt Lake City, I told her the best chance would be out of Big Sandy and sent her on her way.

It was warm with scattered clouds as Ro and I hiked north to Sandpoint Lake and began the four miles to the massive Middle Fork Lake. The moleskin on my heel blisters was bothering me. As I pulled it off, to my horror, my skin stuck to it. Never having had blisters before on a hike, I gazed at the gaping red holes, thinking about the miles ahead. Roanne cut a bagel shape out of a thick piece of moleskin and strapped it over the holes with a bandaid. It worked.

Clouds were building at our backs as the two of us climbed the 11,200-foot divide surrounded by Mt. St. Michel, Dragon-head and Pronghorn Peaks. A flash of lightning and my concern became conscious. A change to warmer clothing and gloves was called for while descending the narrowing valley among yellow buttercups and purple fleabane and finally our ponchos under a light rain. Dove-colored clouds hid the hilltops. Roanne lowered the wet food bags and both of us fell into the tent, happy to be off our feet. The rain stopped. After feasting on couscous and lentil-vegetable curry and washing our dishes, we hung our food, built a fire and sat close, drinking hot peppermint tea. Voices across the creek as a tent went up and the smell of their burning dinner – not alone any longer. An elk bugled in the distance. It started to rain again and continued all night.

Day 4: It was still raining. I was fine until I saw the snow – huge white flakes, exciting at first, except the trail was getting covered very quickly. Our discussion of the possibility of having to walk out and the hazards of staying came to a halt when a call from the direction of the trail pierced the silence. Some hikers approached to see if anybody was home. They weren't taking any chances. It might get socked in for days. A decision to wait until noon was made, and then, if necessary, make the ten-mile walk out.

The people who had arrived last night left. Some hikers from Bonneville Basin left. Roanne didn't want to leave. Neither did I. After carrying all that food up that bloody trail and now, drag it out?

Both of us dozed while the tent sagged, heavy with snow. When I looked out again I couldn't see more than a few feet around us. I deluded myself into thinking there could be blue sky over the ridge but reluctantly came to the realization that it was best to leave. I hated to have to make that decision and felt guilty about it long after the hike.

It was early evening when, after slogging our way out of the mountains, very wet and very tired, Roanne's VW bug came into view. The sky was dark, the mountains, drenched in charcoal clouds. The car stalled and I pushed while she steered and got it started. At the main highway I called to tell Marty that we'd be home early. A man in a pickup helped get the car rolling. It seemed that the car couldn't stop or slow down without stalling. After filling up in Pinedale, it had to be pushed out of the station and at the light in Jackson two kids ran over to help get us rolling.

The forecast was awful for the rest of the week. Snow and more snow. Lucky we got out when we did.

XII

Scab Creek. Again.

August 1993

At the beginning of August Roanne and I left for a walk in the Winds and I forgot my watch. This would be the first trip I wouldn't be able to tell the passing hours during the night, something I relied on when I couldn't sleep. Parked at the Scab Creek Trailhead, again, and with heavy packs and ten days' worth of food, started out. I had to overcome this feeling of fear in the pit of my stomach about not having my Linus blanket. Roanne, always the optimist, suggested I might sleep better without it. That was a possibility. I wasn't going back.

I forgot about it on the uphill trek to Toboggan Lakes which was steep enough to make you forget about everything except putting one foot in front of the other. Since I hadn't done my quota of day hikes to get in shape, I wasn't prepared physically. The muscle spasms started halfway in and I had to stop twice, drop my pack and massage my quivering quads after which Roanne ran me through some stretches. The wooden sign was a welcome sight after nine miles and picking our way through a very swollen south fork under scattered clouds, the last mile was covered to Dream Lake. Lots of bugs.

A light rain forced us indoors for dinner while distant lightning streaked the sky and rumblings of thunder rolled around remote peaks. After hanging our two large plastic bags of food, the two of us wandered until dusk, feeling a need to loosen up after so strenuous a hike, and then built a fire.

On every trip the thought of what drives us into the wilderness comes up. Roanne was raised in the mountains and loves their magic. It's playtime for her. Always answering to others, I need to be alone to feel my own needs. Life is painful at times and our pain can't always be shared. But in the wilderness that pain ebbs because of the infinite space to move through. Nothing is close, there is nothing to hang onto. The forest and high country make me feel alive – fresh air, freedom and raw nature. I need to take risks like sleeping in a tent in bear country. Being adopted and not knowing my roots, I wondered if my forebears were mountain people.

Day 2: In the early hours of the morning a storm tyrannized the valley. As the sky turned light Ro stripped the rainfly halfway and warm sun filtered through the screen. Hot tea. The purified water tasted fishy but the warmth was worth it.

A huge grey cloud hung in the basin while exploring trails radiating from the lake. She and I shared our first apple on the rust-colored, pebbled beach while watching the sky darken and a storm roll in. Hail, then light snow sent us hurrying back to the tent where an enviable afternoon was spent in our sleeping bags adrift in our thoughts. Suddenly the sun surfaced but it was still too cold to stay outdoors. Clouds accumulating on the horizon predicted a cold stormy night.

Day 3: An overcast morning chilled us while hiking the ten miles to Valley Lake. It took most of the day to get there and then find a perfect site. Unexpectedly, a man appeared at our tent, always an intrusion, and asked if there was anybody else with us and how old I was. Embarrassed not to respond, I told him I was fifty-three instead of telling him to mind his own business. I was reminded of my feelings of intimidation, an old story and a bad example for my daughter. It seemed that a white-haired woman was an anachronism in the wilderness. He said he was a Boy Scout leader camping with his six sons across the lake and apologized for having ridden horses in when he heard we had walked. I asked if he could spare some matches since he was leaving the next day. He said he'd drop them by in the morning.

After dinner a stroll around the lake caught him bathing nude. How did he expect us to get around him? Because he was so weird, I got paranoid thinking he might rape us or something. Back at the tent, I placed our cooking pots by the tent opening for him to trip over in case he ventured forth during the night. I laughed at myself but I was apprehensive. I told Roanne how I felt and it was decided to tell him that I had Aids and a gun. The sky cleared as the alpenglow faded on Medina Mountain and stars came out for the first time but we were too exhausted to stay outside and enjoy the night sky.

Day 4: There was frost on the tent and on Roanne's jacket she had left outside. The Boy Scout leader stopped by to leave a box of matches and apologized for his nude bathing. After breakfast a hike into narrow, alpine Europe Canyon to the 11,400-foot pass overlooking the Wind River Indian Reservation and Milky Lakes got us a well-earned lunch. Because a permit was needed to descend to the lakes, the two of us remained on top, surveying the landscape east of the divide – a gentle, rolling green world.

Europe Canyon, Milky Lakes, Wind River Indian Reservation

On the way back to our tent, Roanne picked up a map in a plastic bag that somebody had dropped. It was to supply us with an interesting route on our return – anything to get off the main trail. On a side trip to Long Lake I was enlightened, to say the least, at what Ro called a NOLS identification stamp – their feces spread out on a rock to dry and blow away. She knew about this practice, I didn't appreciate it.

In an attempt to get rid of excess weight, I was burning the pages I had read in my paperback much to Roanne's dismay. I had taught her that books were precious but a few ounces every day added up. After a long twelve-mile day we dropped easily into bed and dozed peacefully during another quiet night.

Day 5: A clear sky welcomed us. At North Fork Lake, the Fremont Trail, a rugged alternative to the Highline stayed above treeline and closer to the Divide. Steep and slow to the top of 10,848-foot Hat Pass. One mile in on the Timico Lake Trail, camp was set up in a thicket of trees on a knoll above the lake. There was time for a walk along the shore to check out the route described on the map Roanne had found. During the night as wind gusts shook the tent, and light rain, thunder and lightning moved overhead, we felt exposed, experienced weird vibes and planned to leave at first light.

Day 6: Back to the Fremont Trail and then north, climbing gradually under a cloudy sky, windy and buggy. The path became less distinct and eventually just cairns marked the way. When those petered out, Ro and I dropped our packs and split up to look around. She glimpsed a lake through the trees far below and from the map it looked like the direction to take.

At the lake she dug a sign out of the bushes that said Baldy Lakes – not on our map. Just as she found a perfect spot, a man approached to see if the site was taken, seemingly one of the only flat places to camp. During the conversation I mentioned the two of us would be walking down to the Fremont Trail in the morning. He said that trail was up not down. As a geologist, the one thing he could do well was read maps and left to get his.

Crouching over his topo map, so much more detailed than ours, I realized that she and I had left the Fremont Trail too early because the second pass did not show up on our map. This was not Bald Mountain Basin where we had planned to be.

After setting up camp and changing to flip-flops Ro and I strolled back "up" to the Fremont Trail and then another three hundred feet to the high pass for a look at the basin that was missed. Because it would be dark within the hour and a storm was moving in, a decision to leave immediately was followed with a promise to return someday. It would not be for another seven years.

Baldy Lake was blissful and a two-night stay was decided upon. All was well until I discovered I had my period. Never having considered it a possibility, being well into menopause, I had brought nothing. I came up with the idea of cutting my Patagonia turtleneck, which had been with me on every trip since moving to Jackson Hole fifteen years ago, into strips and christened them my Patagonia Period Pads. No calcium lactate for cramps but that was the least of my worries. Bears know when a woman is menstruating. I dug a deep hole far from our site for my calls of nature, and while Roanne poured water over my hands, I scrubbed my pads with soap, rinsed them clean, and hung them out to dry. It took a long time and a lot of water, but with nowhere to go and nothing to do, I relaxed into the awareness of my work.

A large fire kept us warm, although our backs stayed cold, while staring into the sky at Cassiopeia, Cepheus, Ursa Minor and Major, Draco, Andromeda, and tried hard for the Great Square. It was too cold to stay out for long and we retired just before a storm moved in. A quiet night with no wind.

Day 7: It was the clearest morning since the beginning of our trip. There were still ambivalent feelings about our decision to stay at the lake rather than moving up to the basin and crossing Angel Pass to the Brown Cliffs and Alpine Lakes, one of the wildest, most remote regions of the Winds. I worried about the high passes and getting down off the Divide because it had been stormy almost every day. Remaining here was certainly safer but was that what we wanted?

After breakfast I talked about my life: why I had done what I did, what motivated me to move on and how I felt being adopted. Was it really any different and, if so, where did that difference lie? After reading all those books about adoption, I had started to feel compassion for the little girl I used to be and what she went through. It was only after I got married and moved away from my parents that I began to listen to my instincts which had eventually led to the divorce. Was I leading the life I wanted or one that my parents had planned for me? It took a few years of married life to figure that out. Did Roanne ever think about the divorce and what she experienced?

Did my mother love me? When Roanne hugged me I felt a warmth I had never experienced before. My mother couldn't handle me, telling me to "wait until your father gets home," so nothing was ever resolved. I wasn't hers and she could only mother me up to a point. My father took on that responsibility. Maybe I was his. Hmmm . . . an interesting thought.

For the first eleven years I lived with the knowledge that my parents were my real parents. Then I was told about my adoption and lived for the next sixty-five years as an adoptee. At the age of seventy-six I was told by an eighty-six-year-old cousin who I had not seen since I was eleven years old that my adoptive father was my biological father. His side of the family had been sworn to secrecy about me being his daughter. Was that because of an affair he had and wanted to keep from my adoptive mother? Why else would it have been kept as such a deep, dark secret? None of the psychics I had visited could penetrate the veil. Did my adoptive mother know I was my father's daughter? If she did she never let on.

It was windy and chilly even though the sun was out but a walk around the lake on white sand, wading in tepid, calf-high water was relaxing.

Another try for Bald Mountain Basin and Angel Pass found us leaving cairns, being off trail, to mark the way. Each time the top of a hill was gained, there was another to climb and the pass which looked very steep wasn't getting any closer. It was almost dark when our tent came into view. Too tired for dinner, some ramen was easy after which we built a fire as evening shadows beckoned the cold.

Day 8: Heading south, closing the loop, and because the sky was clear, a decision was made to try that alternate route on the map. Hiking down to the Bell Lakes Trail, up two miles to the Timico cutoff, and a climb to the saddle southwest of Round Top Mountain found us in deep snow. At the top a packer took our picture while his mule, Ruby, rested from the long climb. She sank to her knees as they descended and quickly disappeared into the trees.

It was late afternoon when we picked up the new Highline Trail to Lake Vera, our next campsite, but didn't feel comfortable in such closed quarters and continued on, trying desperately to get above treeline. Seven and a half miles later, at dusk, a sign emerged out of the gloom that could barely be read, Junction Lake. Much to our surprise, it was very close to our final destination, Dream Lake. Exhausted and too dark to go on, I set up the tent while Roanne ran back to the creek to get some water because the lake below was swampy; too tired to eat anything but a cup of hot soup. If there would be anywhere in the Winds for bears, it would be here, Roanne remarked. It took me awhile to fall asleep.

Day 9: "Look! No one's here!" I said as I peeked out of the tent in the early morning. "Who wants to be? We're in a swamp. They should have named this Swamp Lake!" exclaimed Roanne. A clear day welcomed us and hiking the four miles to Dream Lake with our swampy socks hanging from our packs, drying, was easy. Worn out from yesterday, the tent went up in our familiar spot and Roanne fell asleep. A late afternoon stroll to Raid Lake where the two of us sat on rocks jutting into the middle of the water, and walked in sand, so comforting to our feet. A huge fire kept us warm that evening and I finished and burned the last pages of my book.

Day 10: A clear morning except for some stratus clouds to the north and mixed feelings as ever upon leaving. It was a long walk out. The parking lot was almost empty. Emerging from the wilderness was always a shock, but wonderful to take off boots, peel off socks and relax in true fulfillment, *a fait accompli,* an ephemeral feeling, an enduring memory.

XIII

Egypt Lake

A quick summary of the past five years: my parents died within two years; Roanne made it to Europe; I was immersed in searching for my birth mother; the black market baby scandal of which I was a part, hit the news; both my older daughters got married and my oldest became pregnant; I became a grandmother; received an invitation to visit the Wyoming Governor's Mansion; our Kelly, Wyoming cabin burned down and we were living in Canada full-time; purchased a small house in Calgary for Ro to live in and us to visit when supplies were needed; Marty, as a film director, was asked to shoot a film in Boulder, Colorado; babysat a friend's home in Hawaii where I discovered I had the beginnings of cancer and cured myself with the help of a Hawaiian Kahuna.

August 1998:
The skies had been clear for weeks but when Roanne and I left our cabin in Golden, British Columbia at 8:00 a.m., it was foggy. A light drizzle turned to steady rain after Lake Louise but at the Sunshine Area turnoff, voluminous white clouds allowed brief glimpses of blue. At the start of the trail a park employee cheerfully told us about a bear that had been seen on Healy Pass where the two of us were headed. She wished us luck and hoped we might catch a glimpse of him.

Roanne and I had decided to spend a few days at Egypt Lake, one of the most beautiful and popular areas in Banff National Park. The trail, 7.8 miles, gradually ascended the Healy Creek Valley through dense Engelmann spruce and alpine fir to a campground where a stop for a snack was welcomed. After four miles of steady uphill hiking, scattered earth piles appeared in meadows where the bear had been digging for roots. The last alpine larches were left behind as 7,650-foot Healy Pass loomed ahead and an unforgettable view of 9,376-foot Mt. Bourgeau, 11,578-foot Mt. Assiniboine, the Matterhorn of the Rockies, 9,293-foot Monarch and the long ridge extending from its flanks to Healy Pass known as the Monarch Ramparts.

West of this windy pass, the flat steel-blue contoured cutouts of Egypt and Scarab Lakes appeared, nestled in the forested valley beneath the Pharaoh Peaks. While lost in a landscape of shadows and shapes, lunch was enjoyed. A passing warden informed us that the grizzly was around, had followed some hikers, but hadn't bothered anybody yet. Yet? I brought out my bear bell!

The trail dropped rapidly to the campground. After checking the empty sites, the furthest one looked best, our tent was set up, our stuff stashed, and our food hung on the high bear bars, an ingenious device that had a number of cables onto which you could clip your food bag and hoist it about twenty feet. No more throwing rocks over tree branches. This was a Park, not the wilderness. After filtering and filling our containers with water from the creek below, dinner was prepared just as it started to drizzle. Here we were again, by ourselves, catching up on mother-daughter stuff not dealt with down below.

A shelter cabin built in 1969 that could sleep sixteen back-packers was located in the middle of the campground and I thought how safe I would feel sleeping there, although I didn't really like being indoors in the mountains. The wind, rain, and night noises are soothing, although the hoarse grunting of a grizzly wasn't. A light rain lulled us to sleep.

Day 2: A cold morning was alleviated with a breakfast of hot oatmeal and a climb up the steep switchbacks to the cirques above Egypt Lake; passed Scarab Lake and continued through light hail, scrambling up a rocky track towards Mummy Lake, rimmed by tundra and talus. Seeking cover under a tree, lunch was savored while snow fell around us. On our way back, a rocky gorge overhanging Egypt Lake sheltered us from the wind and our homemade oat bars warmed us while watching cloud shadows crawl over a treed landscape. We bushwhacked down to the lake, ready for a dinner of quinoa, lentils and vegetables, then walked to the shelter cabin and, sitting by the woodstove, talked to a young French couple hitch-hiking across Canada.

Day 3: In the early morning hours, the wind rose and picked up in volume as the sun filtered through the trees, creating an evergreen pattern on the tent. I meditated. It was cloudy and cold when I finally got the courage to slip out of my comfortable cocoon and look outside. After cooking breakfast and warming up in the shelter, Ro and I left for a fifteen-mile loop up Whistling Valley, a staggering gap between the Pharaoh Peaks and the precipitous slopes of the Great Divide to Shadow Lake and back along the creek.

Climbing the switchbacks again Ro and I continued the steady ascent to rugged, rocky Whistling Pass, where marmots whistled their warnings to passersby. In the distance, heavenly Haiduk Lake was nestled in the dell far below the cliffs of the Ball Range. The steep trail twisted down to marshy meadows alongside the lake and then, quite steeply, through subalpine forest to Shadow Lake. A light rain continued while hiking the muddy path to the backcountry lodge where lunch was devoured on the porch. Back at Egypt Lake, 6:30 p.m., and lucky to be able to dry our boots by the woodstove after dinner.

It suddenly turned very cold and a decision was made to sleep in the cabin. After hot tea the two of us climbed into bed – a plywood platform much less comfortable than the ground. At either end of the main room that housed the wood stove, common cooking area, tables and benches, were two smaller chambers, each with four bunks, upper and lower. Lucky for us to have one of the rooms to ourselves until 6:00 a.m. when a cold camper stumbled into the cabin. Roanne and I got up to pee, started a fire in the stove, and quickly got back into our bags – a soft thank you sounded from one of the sleepy occupants in the end room.

After breakfast a hike up the short steep few miles to Pharaoh and Black Rock Lakes was invigorating. Finding Sphinx

Lake proved impossible and a hesitant return was made to Black Rock for lunch in the sun. A hiker passed, also unable to find the lake.

Back at the shelter the warden ticketed us for having spent the night indoors, not a fine but a $5 fee each per bunk, cheap lodgings but then they were far from luxurious. Our cold tent under clear skies was not welcome, but dinner helped to warm us. Roanne fell asleep quickly while I listened to the Universe breathing.

It was very cold during the night. Towards morning, as black turned to grey, I awoke to the sound of footsteps and froze in my bag. It was a long few seconds before I realized that somebody was packing up to leave early. Tea and oat squares were enjoyed on the cabin steps in hot sun while our rainfly dried. Everybody who was walking out that day had already left.

Just before 10:00 a.m. the two-mile climb to Healy Pass began. It took just under an hour. The rest of the hike was downhill and, arriving at the bottom at 1:30 p.m., we soaked our sore feet in the creek while talking about our trip.

There seems to be more camaraderie in the backcountry here in Canada than in most other places where I have backpacked. It could be because of the shelter cabins and backcountry lodges where people congregate. But these are National Parks not wilderness. I have never touched wilderness in the far north.

Note: Why Egypt? The two pyramid-shaped Pharaoh Peaks overlooking the lakes had been previously named and A. O. Wheeler, founder of the Alpine Club of Canada, decided to stick with the Egyptian theme in the Egypt Lake Valley.

XIV

Tonquin Valley

September 1998:

Roanne wished to "get away from it all" and had found a job cooking at a lodge in the Purcell Peaks, outside of Golden and remote enough that it required her to be helicoptered in. I never needed much of an excuse to go for a hike in the wilderness, even though we already lived in what most people would call wilderness – a log cabin on eighty acres, off-grid, was not exactly city living. But there was something about walking into the mountains carrying all you need for a few days in paradise.

She had always wanted to hike into the Tonquin Valley in Jasper National Park and see the Ramparts. The only thing that kept me out of that park was its notorious reputation for grizzlies. That's why hiking in Yellowstone, just ninety miles north of our cabin in Kelly (Jackson Hole), was never an option.

With the crowds and heat of summer past, Roanne and I packed up on September 7th, drove west to Lake Louise and picked up the Icefields Parkway, one of the most majestic drives in the world, north to Jasper. At Saskatchewan Crossing a smoky haze caused some concern. At the Columbia Icefield, the largest chain of icefields along the Divide and origin of many mighty rivers that run to the Pacific, the Canadian prairies and the Arctic Ocean, a stop was made to ask about fires. Two, both west of Jasper, were causing the fog, depending on which way the wind was blowing. I asked my invariable question about bears. "There have been numerous bluff charges by grizzlies in the Tonquin Valley but no encounters. You might want to change your plans." I took a deep breath and looked at Roanne. She didn't care but knew I did. "We can always go somewhere else, Ma!"

My fear of bears took second place to my need to please my daughter. All she had talked about were the Ramparts and that's where she and I were going, bears or no bears. The two of us had been hiking in bear country for twenty years. Why should this be any different?

The town of Jasper was bustling with tourists at 4:00 p.m. There was a grizzly warning but bluff charges were unheard of. "After all, we're the ones who would know," said this self-important park ranger. With four campgrounds to pick from, the Clitheroe site was recommended as "the best of the bunch" and it was reserved for two nights. Since lodging was needed for the night and I couldn't book anything without a credit card, the manager of the Edith Clavell Hostel promised to hold two bunks until 6:00 p.m., giving us forty minutes for some quick grocery shopping and the twenty-nine kilometer drive to the hostel, fourteen of them up a rough, narrow, switchbacked road.

At one minute to six Ro pulled into the parking lot and found that nobody had called ahead to hold our spot. However, this place was anything but full. The manager, a retired French-Canadian from Quebec, showed us around and explained how things worked – the recycling bins, fridge protocol, where to dump dishwater, drinking water had to be boiled, and which outhouse was off-limits. The sewage was supposed to have been picked up that afternoon and because the crew had still not appeared, he apologized for the smell and boasted about running a clean place, "the best in the Rockies." I knew that meant trouble. "No bears have ever come around," he said. They probably couldn't stand the smell.

The ladies' dorm was occupied by an elderly gentleman who had slept with his wife the previous night because there was nobody else in the room. But now there were other women in the building and still he hadn't been asked to move to the men's dorm. Our host couldn't explain why when I asked. Roanne and I chose bunks, transferred our packs to the dorm because the stench in the parking lot made it impossible to unpack in the car, and brought our food into the kitchen to start dinner. There was a strange feeling about the place and we would have eaten outside at a picnic table but for the smell.

Two elderly women prepared dinner while their husbands complained about having to help. One of the men left the door open every time he entered or left which caused the smell to permeate the inside. I finally got up and slammed the door shut but nobody noticed. A family of six waited while the woman of the group set the table and prepared the food. Nobody helped as she walked around the table making sure everything was in place. A young man who had been reading outside secured a corner of the floor and kept reading. A totally incongruous group and we ate among strangers.

After dinner our food bags were labeled and dated and placed in the overcrowded fridge, most of the room taken up with beer and wine. Deciding a short hike was essential rather than hanging around until dark, the two kilometers to the end of the road brought us to the glacier and ice caves under Mt. Edith Clavell's spectacular north face. It was dusk upon our return. Ro and I arranged our bunks for the night and sat outside at a blazing bonfire, talking for an hour or so with a German family whose offer of marshmallows we declined. They came from a tiny village on the German-Swiss-Austrian border, had lived there all their lives, and were visiting the parks in British Columbia. They remarked on how many Germans they had met during their travels in Canada.

After a long day, the two of us were looking forward to an uninterrupted and comfortable night's sleep, neither of which happened. The man in the far bunk snored continuously, the lady near him tossed and turned on a noisy plastic mattress cover and the young girl at the other end kept turning on her light to check the time. Roanne had stayed in many hostels around the world and said this was the worst. It was my first.

Day 2: The sky was clear but when I went outside to pee at 2:00 a.m., there were a few clouds around the peaks; at 5:00 a.m., it was overcast; and at 7:00 a.m., it was raining lightly. A faint feeling of relief: I wouldn't have to face the bears.

After dressing quickly and quietly packing up, Ro started breakfast in the hostel kitchen while I used their cell phone to call for the weather forecast: 60% chance of rain with afternoon thundershowers today; 40% chance of the same for the next two days. I didn't want to walk seventeen kilometers into grizzly country in the rain, and Roanne had to struggle to put up with me. She let me do my thing, get through my fear and luxurious illusions that involved a drive back to town to try and change our plans.

By the time we reached Jasper the sun was out. The attendant suggested another hike but because there was a penalty to change reservations, both of us hesitated. She said she'd forgo it, commendable for a government employee to come to such a decision on her own. Ro and I sat on the front steps of the building discussing our dilemma. Because of a high pass and the inclement weather, the Skyline Trail was not a good compromise. I decided the grizzlies over the high trail were the lesser of two evils and Roanne drove back to the hostel. She was very patient, so sensitive. That's why these trips were comfortable and necessary, a reciprocity in our relationship.

Warned about the five kilometers of strenuous switchbacks at the end of the hike, our packs were stripped down to the barest essentials and the two of us finally started the seventeen-kilometer walk, having already lost two hours. Heading for the high country where the air was crisp and clear, the wildflowers, what was left of them, brilliant and a feeling of grandeur enhanced pristine peaks and expansive valleys.

The first eight kilometers, a long gradual descent along the forested north slope of Mt. Edith Clavell, were easy; walked along the Astoria River most of the way, the express route to the Tonquin Valley; passed two couples with their bells ringing, none of whom had seen a bear. I let my bell ring even though it bothered Roanne who had the wonderful capacity to walk in bear country without a worry. I didn't. In fact that was all I thought about.

The switchbacks up Old Horn Mountain weren't too steep, and it was a surprise to reach the top so quickly. The Amethyst

Lakes at the base of the Ramparts, a 3000-foot wall of
Precambrian quartz sandstone making up ten spectacular
castellated peaks, reminded us of Titcomb Basin in the Wind
Rivers. The feeling of being on the roof of the world permeated
places like these, and the excitement sent my blood rushing and
made my head light.

The Ramparts

It took three more long kilometers to reach the campground
only to find it in dense forest and far from the lake with no water
nearby. I found it hard to believe that it was two more kilometers
down to the lake for water and then back up again. A room with
a view, promised by the park attendant, was not to be had.
Bitching and moaning while setting up camp and hanging our
food, a decision was made to hike the kilometer to the warden's
cabin far below.

Trish, the warden, was surprised to hear that nobody told us
water was 300 meters north of the campground. However, there
was another site in the middle of the valley that might be
preferable, and suggested a walk, only one more kilometer, to
check it out before she called to change our reservations.

Surprise Point was made to order. She radioed headquarters and found it was available for the next two nights. Returning to our site, the two of us struck camp and walked the last two kilometers of the day to our new quarters, adding another six to our seventeen, a long day with a full pack. At fifty-seven I couldn't carry what I used to when I was forty-two.

The Ramparts, Amethyst Lake

Dinner was prepared while watching the clouds sink into the canyons. After hanging our food again, Ro and I dressed warmly and hiked to the lakeshore where I sketched the valley until the light faded. Our tent was familiar, a home away from home, and I arranged my interior side pocket with everything I needed for the long night ahead. Suddenly realizing that Marty's birthday was three days from now, the two of us decided to walk out on Thursday to be in time for a Friday Indian buffet at our favorite restaurant.

Roanne had wanted to do this trip because she had something on her mind. She said we pretend a lot, don't really talk, and it distressed her. She wanted a good relationship with me and felt she and I didn't have one and hadn't for a long time. Oh, God! What now! She was the closest of my three daughters and I needed a moment to think about this – anything to take my mind off bears.

She said I treated her like a child, asking her things to which I knew the answers. I guess I did it when I had nothing to say and felt the need to communicate. I was still mothering her; she was thirty years old, and it made her angry and short with me. I, in turn, became insecure, feeling rejected by her, probably an established pattern from my mother and me. Both of us wanted to be friends but this behavior got in the way. I cried a bit while talking about her sisters, my estranged daughters. She thought I had to let them go. So did I. But how?

It was after midnight when she fell asleep. I loved to lie in our tent while raindrops landed gently on the nylon rainfly, sounding like a needle pricking taut fabric. At 4:30 a.m. I awoke to two grunts. I waited without breathing, not moving. A third grunt. I froze not wanting the rustle of the sleeping bag to whisper a warning. I must have dozed because it was suddenly 8:45 a.m. and I realized it had stopped raining. I opened the rainfly to see the mountains draped in white and the valley floor glistening wet.

Day 2: Dressed in every piece of clothing in our packs, our hunger drove us to retrieve our food. As the cables were released, a motion in the far meadow caught our eyes. It moved like a moose but didn't have that distinctive profile. Trish had told us of a herd of upland caribou that roamed the valley. Maybe the grunts were theirs. Sure they were.

Roanne made some tea and, sitting in the sun to get warm, both of us gazed at our surroundings. Back at the tent, still in shadow, we climbed into our sleeping bags and while listening to the roar of cracking ice high in the crevices of glaciers and tumbled rocks, Roanne read some of her poetry – such depths of despair. Does she suffer so? Was this my daughter? I felt guilty but denied it because it would be too hard to live with. Her life was her responsibility, but the divorce was mine. This hypersensitive being wasn't as happy as I would have liked her to be. Was I? I was when walking in the mountains. I was sure my love for the alpine must be reminiscent of my family of origin. Almost two decades later when I discovered that my adoptive father was my biological father I had to rearrange my thinking about myself as to whom I am. My father was an ardent fisherman and was never happier than when he was out in the wilderness, fishing.

Tired from our long walk the day before, plans to walk into Eremite Valley were scrapped for a leisurely day hiking around the lakes. The clouds were building around the peaks, slowly crawling into the valley, and I knew the two of us were in for another cold night. Without enough sun to be comfortable, a return to a warm tent was necessary. It was drizzling lightly while Roanne slept and I thought about Marty, looking forward to our walk out tomorrow. The weather wasn't promising and I was glad not to be staying longer.

Without a book I had my thoughts to ponder. I had always assumed that most of my life had been happy, but now I wondered. Denial is a great mechanism and can lead one to believe anything. How many moments in our lifetimes were really filled with joy? Why didn't it last? The Buddha said the essence of life was suffering and a well-disciplined mind brought happiness. Meditation was intended to purify the mind and so I planned to go on a silent retreat for a week of yoga and meditation. Roanne would be cooking for the group, as she had done for the past two years, and said it would do me good. If I dyed my hair and used wrinkle-free creams, I would say my age bothered me. It did to some extent but I would rather watch it creep up then be surprised one day at my graying roots and loose skin. I didn't feel I had contributed much to mankind: in my art and writing – maybe some. Had my adoption been a cause of suffering? How could I tell? I was eight years into a search for my birth parents. I guess that says it all.

During the night the wind in the peaks left the trees and tent undisturbed. During the evening another tent had moved in. The man inside snored for a few hours and I found it comforting, thinking it would keep the bears away.

Day 3: It was very cold. Someone was scurrying around taking pictures of the alpenglow on the Ramparts. Roanne started some tea while I struck camp. At 9:00 a.m., walking south on a rough, rocky trail, the two of us descended the two kilometers to the head of Eremite Valley and stopped for water and some almonds while I sketched a large beautiful mushroom at the side of the path.

mushroom

Six kilometers to the log bridge that crossed the Astoria River and another eight to the car. The ringing of bells heralded the approach of hikers. I had put my bells away until Ro heard a loud crack in the woods and asked me to get them out.

Clavell Lake marked the end of our journey and a dunk in its frigid water left Roanne breathless. Climbing the bank to the car she and I drove back to Jasper for some gas and a cold beer, feeling a lot closer than before. That's what our walks were all about. Perhaps the mountains in their steadfastness provide the security and freedom needed to allow us to let go, admit, open the gates to the worries and fears we deny while living in our insecure, judgmental world.

I called Marty to tell him we'd be home in time to celebrate his birthday.

122

A Queen

May 2000

...in our life, the mountains
in our life, streams, fields, tree
Oh the beautiful trees.
Remember, the life you saved?
Always, in our life, freedom
to meander the edges of our minds
branded boundaries with lakes
They held our image...

> I knew this lady
> and she knew me
> we grew up together
> though we are not sisters
> but we might as well be

...of a sacred tryst
invisible, embedded with jewels
of loss, shadows and rain.
Always, in our life, laughter, dreams
travel
In our life, walks in the mountains,
losing reality in valleys, plateaus,
and tent-talk...

> her many lined hand
> cradles every soul
> like a child
> she seeks comfort
> in the unfolding, and in the old

...in our life, always, the mountains
the mist of native incense,
the mouth sweetened with song

Oh, the music, ne'er a dull moment
Always, in our life, sun sparkled lakes
accompanying lunch, on a rock
Always, time.
Always one more corner, hill, turn...

this gestation
of her disclosure
as soft as a rose
timely as a train
she announced her birth

...she allowed me to lead her
and carry her, she allowed me to change
but not without skepticism
she made me want to live.
She taught me her delicate balance
In our life, always so much to do,
there is water to get, wood to chop
garden to till, birds to feed...

the same hands create,
the same tear
a comfortable life,
She wears the remnants
beautifully adorned, a queen.

Happy Mother's Day

Love, Roanne

XV

The Wind Rivers

I loved the silent retreat and did another a year later; Roanne was off to Hawaii on a much deserved vacation; my art exhibit in Calgary went well; I became a grandmother for the second time; Marty and I visited the Kushi Institute in Brookline, Massachusetts and started macrobiotics; my Certificate of Judgment, a confirmation of my adoption, was finally found after searching for 10 years; Marty and I tied the knot after twenty-seven years; Roanne now in her early thirties, has begun to question her past after living on her own for many years.

August 2000:

Roanne was finishing her work at the Kushi Institute campus in Becket, Massachusetts and mentioned, on one of our long distance calls that she wanted to go for a hike in late August. At her suggestion of the Winds, I became excited. We hadn't walked in the Wind Rivers for the last seven years since moving to Canada. When Karen heard of our plan, she wanted to join us. I instantly thought if Maxine were with us, I would have my three daughters back together again. Wishful thinking. I fell so easily into denying we had been estranged for twenty-five years.

As the weeks slipped by, Karen's interest waned and she finally reneged. A visit with her father and her cancellation had coincided.

Roanne and her current boyfriend, on his way to Oregon, were driving across Canada from Massachusetts and would stop at our cabin for a few days before he continued on and she and I headed south for Wyoming.

The West was drier than it had been in years. I called the Outdoor Shop in Pinedale and learned that two nearby fires were almost under control. Elkhart Park was closed as well as the south entrance to Yellowstone, and there was a large burn just outside of Dubois, nowhere near our direction.

After thirteen hours on the road, Roanne and I pulled into our friend's driveway in Jackson and unloaded our gear onto her living room floor. Bonnie watched in awe as our food was figured out for the trip, our backpacks packed and our age-old list, checked off, making sure everything was in order. She wanted to try on our packs to see what it was like and was satisfied to discover that this was nothing she ever wanted to do. Our car was loaded, her offer of a tiny radio to hear the weather reports was turned down and the two of us climbed into bed, too weary and restless for sleep.

Day 1: In Hoback Canyon, ten miles south of Jackson, fire-fighting camps lined the highway and heavy smoke obscured the landscape. As the haze cleared, two sandhill cranes materialized in a meadow and watched us drive by, unconcerned at all the activity around them.

The day was clear, warm, and slightly windy when Ro parked the car in a meadow where cows and their calves watched as the two of us crossed timidly (Roanne has been chased by cows before) and started hiking up the ridge on an unmarked trail until it disappeared; making our way through an old burn, a stop for a snack on a deadfall pine before picking up the path only to lose it again. The going was extremely difficult and my legs were becoming badly scratched climbing over fallen trees and struggling through underbrush, balancing our heavy packs, getting very tired and dejected because the trail couldn't be found.

Rex, owner of the Outdoor Shop in Pinedale, had told us about this shortcut, saying Burnt Lake could be seen to our right and to stay high on the ridge. The two of us couldn't figure out why our compass registered south when heading north. Well into the afternoon Roanne was tempted to turn back and head for another entrance. I considered that a good idea.

We decided to drop our packs and scramble up the hillside for another look; another ridge and more trees worried us.

Although the Wind River peaks could finally be seen in the distance, where was the Timico Lake Trail? Exhausted and disheartened, the thought of camping at the bottom of a steep, congested ravine was dropped after choosing to hike up once more for another look. Roanne ran ahead and minutes after disappearing over the top I heard her excited yell that she had found a trail – a real trail with hoof and boot prints.

Energized by the joy of discovery, the two of us pressed on, passing broken-down Black's cabins at Belford Lake, towards Lake Jacqueline, where it was said there was good camping. Roanne found a beautiful spot ringed with trees already in shadow. It took minutes for our tent to go up, then much longer to hang our heavy bags of food. My university physics came in handy and I moved up the hill, so the angle wasn't so acute, and while Roanne held the bag and gave it a final heave, I pulled it up.

It was twilight when she heated water for tea after the last of our rice rolls from lunch were devoured. Our sleeping bags warmed our chilled bodies as Ro and I stretched out, thankful to be where we were. My shoulders were sore, my calves scratched raw, and tender hip bones kept me on my back while I experienced a condition well beyond exhaustion. Roanne fell asleep while I listened to the sounds of the wilderness.

Suddenly a far-off rumbling shattered the serenity. I lay still and listened. There it was again, a bit closer. It wasn't long before lightning lit up the tent and the first drops sizzled on our rainfly. This was our first night in our new tent and a good way to test its efficiency. Thunder ripped the air, crackled, groaned and rumbled overhead while lightning never let up. It rained for about a half-hour, welcoming us back to the Winds and outdoor life.

Day 2: Heading towards Barnes and Chain Lakes, the Baldy Lakes Trail and our next campsite. The two of us had been here in 1993, seven years ago when looking for Bald Mountain Basin and mistakenly ended up at Baldy Lakes. Mt. Baldy loomed ahead and approaching the turnoff, a yellow tent near the wooden sign made us wonder why these hikers camped in such an exposed site. A climb of six hundred feet over two miles brought us to the cutoff for the Lakes – hot sun, sparse clouds and short gusts of wind – and with only a mile to go, all up, Ro and I turned into the narrow bosky canyon.

When our packs were finally lowered to the ground, I noticed that my rubber flip-flops were gone. When I had tied them to my backpack this morning, I had a fleeting thought that I should have clipped them onto the strap. Why don't I listen to my instincts? Roanne lent me hers but I couldn't imagine spending the rest of the trip without mine.

The tent pitched, our gear stashed, and, although very tired, a hike to the head of the valley to stretch our legs was achieved. It was wonderful walking without weight. While cleaning our pots at the lake, a hiker came by and I asked if he had seen a pair of flip-flops on the trail. I was surprised when he said he had and knew Roanne thought me mad when I decided to retrieve them. With twenty minutes until sundown, I was off, running down the twisting trail into the treed gully, dodging rocks and deadfall. There they were. I was back with my bounty as the canyon dipped into soft, purple-grey shadow.

Was it a bugling elk or a yelping coyote that was heard when climbing into our sleeping bags at the end of another long day? The ground was lumpy and I changed sides with Roanne because, as she said, she could sleep on anything, an amazing faculty when it came to camping. I slept for two-hour intervals during the calm, starry night, but my pondering didn't match the peacefulness of my surroundings.

I thought about a dream I'd had a few years ago. I had a child, left it, and when I returned, the realization as to what I had done left me chilled. The image had clung to my consciousness. Then Roanne told me what Michio Kushi (Kushi Institute of Macrobiotics) had said when asked about adoption during their talks on ancestry and roots. If a person neglected a child in one of their past lives, it would be the reason for them to be adopted this time around so as to experience "neglect." The word "neglect" was disturbing and left me feeling worthless.

Day 3: Stayed in bed until the sun came up and talked about our pasts. I had tears when I reminisced about leaving my daughters behind, and Roanne spoke about how alone and miserable she was after coming West without her sisters. All of us were except that Marty and I had an escape – smoking pot made our burden easier to bear. She knew that when the two of us smoked she'd be on her own and hated it. I told her it made us more creative and she thought that was true. But it was an addiction and answered a deeper need. More tears. Hearing her account of our marijuana use made me feel guilty and in an effort to explain, I told her I couldn't deal with my life back then. She and I had never discussed our real feelings after the divorce.

I talked about the first trip back East to see my parents in Montreal after having been gone for years, and how, when I asked about my adoption, my mother spoke excitedly about the day I arrived while my father stared into his plate and finally stopped her; and how after asking him time and again about my adoption he swore he knew nothing. I hated them at the time and Roanne was surprised to hear me speak so candidly.

My journal:
> *Two women in the woods*
> *With their necessary goods*
> *Talking truths, admitting lies*
> *From childhood years, times gone by*
> *Tears of grief rolled down my cheeks*
> *The sun rose over mountain peaks.*

A waterfall tumbling through a rocky hillside gully across from our campsite beckoned and I sketched our tent, minute against the massive mountainside while Roanne dozed. Nobody ventured into the valley all day. The battery to my watch died during the evening and again I couldn't tell when daylight was due, always a comfort. Roanne recalled having a time window on her camera, so all that had to be done was find out what time it was and then figure out how to set it. It took another few days for that to happen.

Baldy Lakes

Day 4: Packed up and climbed to the open, grassy slopes of the 10,840-foot saddle overlooking broad, wild Bald Mountain Basin, searched for a site in this vast, barren, rocky realm dotted with small ponds and lakes and finally made a choice. The lake just below our site was murky and water was filtered from another. I shared Roanne's *ume-sho-kuzu* drink, a soothing macrobiotic mixture that aided digestion by stimulating the intestines and alkalizing the system. She fell asleep in the afternoon while I sketched the angel's wings. Something had changed between us. She seemed distant

Bald Mountain Basin, Angel Pass

Excerpt from Roanne's journal: *I knew something was going to happen. I was impatient, carrying a remark she made yesterday in my gut, unable to voice how I felt. Why can't I just say something and relieve this pressure?*

While sitting on the rock by our tent, watching the mauve and red streaked sky dissolve to dark grey, the two of us talked about a walk tomorrow and decided to let the weather dictate our direction. It got chilly quickly and after storing our food in her backpack, wrapping it in a rubber poncho with a plastic garbage bag pulled over it, and placing it against a rock because there were no trees, she and I retired to the tent.

I mentioned that I didn't like some of the things I had done in the past and that in my writing, these issues were coming up, forcing me finally to deal with them. I found her disinterested, her questions vague and intimidating, and when I attempted to answer them she impatiently cut me off, saying she had heard all the stories before. I stopped talking.

Excerpt from Roanne's journal: *"Is there something wrong?" Mom asked, her age and experience giving strength to ease this moment, this crucial opening to matters of the heart. "Yes," I said, as if caught. In the darkness tears ladled from the well of my windburned eyes, my throat swelled and in bitter accusations, I brought up our past in avoidance of what really was on my mind – another boyfriend of mine falling short, of what she says, I deserve. I didn't want to let her in, but wished to hurl every one of her wrongdoings in her face. I wanted to make her feel her mistakes in order for my problems to be justified. She broke from the norm following a dream. I know it saved any vestige of happiness she could have in this life. My sisters still blamed her . . . did I? How am I to open my heart if I can't be up front with the one woman who has been my best friend since before time? Is it worth blaming, still, the shortcomings and hard knocks her gentle soul has endured . . . and mine?*

Roanne talked about a visit to Martha's Vineyard with her father and sisters just after the divorce, a disturbing time for me.

I was surprised at hearing the whole story, so different from what she had recounted before. She suddenly asked why I had never gone for therapy. During the separation I had gone to get some questions answered. The psychologist told me I needn't come back, that I knew quite clearly what I was doing. After my visit, I took the children to the therapist because of their hostility towards each other and me.

I felt threatened about being challenged as to why I did the things I did. She fell asleep and I cried. I was using more tissues than had been planned for and worried about running out. I wanted to go home. I didn't need this trip anymore. What I needed was good feelings, and if the two of us couldn't be supportive of one another, why push being together?

Roanne had wanted to come on this hike and talk, having been apart for almost two years. Perhaps this was the wrong time. She had a boyfriend and I could understand her preferring to be with him. However, during all our telephone calls, she had persisted in making plans with me. So here we were – estranged. She seemed withdrawn and impatient. I was beginning to experience that old feeling of rejection. She complained of being tired, saying she might be doing too much and should have stayed in Calgary (Canada) longer to rest up. But we didn't have that luxury. The mountains would be inaccessible soon because summer was at its end. Maybe both of us should just go home!

She was sleeping and I was upset. Whenever I talked about the divorce I got stressed. I didn't like to make excuses. She was blaming me just as her sisters had, and I felt defensive as I repeated the same old stories. Here I was after twenty-five years with the same awful feelings and that knot in my gut. I tried to remember the truth of what happened, devoid of laminated blame, hatred and guilt. I didn't leave my two older daughters – they left me. For whatever reasons and I knew they thought they had good ones, they had made the choice to remain with their father.

I was shocked and felt victimized when Roanne accused me of getting rid of her and her sisters when I sent them to camp for part of the summer during the divorce. Where had that come from? I didn't remember feeling that way and it bothered me. She put doubts in my mind. Did it bother me because it was true? What I did recall was my desire to get the girls out of the turmoil of the times so that they could enjoy some of their summer vacation. More tears and more treasured toilet paper. My nose was blocked and I continuously had to blow it, hoping perhaps that the noise would wake her up so the air could be cleared. Suddenly in the stillness . . .

Excerpt from Roanne's journal: *"Are you okay, Ma?" "I want to go home," she blurted out, crying hard. My heart burst. Look what you did, a little voice inside said. I hurt the only person I love more than life itself and blamed her for something I cannot face – rejection.* The two of us *talked into the night releasing some of the pain.*

I told Roanne I was angered when she accused me of wanting to get rid of my kids by sending them to camp. I felt terrible at her questioning me about not going for therapy. I worried that she was tired and I had pushed for the hike. I was miserable and I wanted to go home. She calmly cut through my anxiety by suggesting that maybe she and I came into the mountains because we needed to talk it out, whatever "it" was, and I suddenly relaxed, realizing I could let go of the victim role. She said she pushed my buttons until I broke in order to instigate a confrontation. She needed to talk about something and forced me into bringing it about. Okay, so what did I need to face?

She resented the fact that I accused her of going with a guy who had cancer, another stupid-men-choice as she put it. What I felt strange about was that he hadn't told her and she had to find out from a friend. That had precipitated the feelings I expressed about her boyfriend and had shaped my thoughts about his character. I was just a mother concerned with her daughter's happiness and this was an issue that had to be faced. She felt I was disappointed in her. I wasn't. Didn't it bother her that he wasn't being honest?

I then voiced my concern about crossing the Divide and possibly getting stranded on the other side, but I didn't want to spoil our plans to climb Angel Pass and see the Brown Cliffs and Alpine Lakes that she and I had been talking about for years. At this time of the year storms could move in that might endanger us, having faced that years ago when forced out of the Winds in early September because of snow.

I didn't want to talk about my divorce anymore because as much as I tried to deal with it, I still couldn't. I cried and we talked. We talked and I cried. I felt guilty about Roanne sleeping on the uneven side, having changed because she said she could sleep anywhere but then complained about it being lumpy. I was paranoid about having left the car in a meadow rather than at a marked trailhead, wondering if it could be found again and if there was danger of encroaching fires.

Both of us worried about the walk out and didn't want to repeat the difficulties experienced on the way in. I cried some more and the two of us talked on, finally deciding that neither of us wanted to push so hard. Having arranged an aggressive hike – crossing the Divide twice, late in the season with heavy packs – stressed us out, each not wanting to disappoint the other.

Emotionally spent after baring our souls, I had to pee and Roanne accompanied me into the cold night air. Back in my bag I shook pretty badly for a while. I was wrung out. A half-moon had risen from behind the left wing of Angel Pass and the stars were out, promising a clear day ahead. It must have been near morning when Ro and I finally fell asleep.

Excerpt from Roanne's journal: *The sky was turning apricot and pink. Angel Pass sank its ragged wings into a cold morning sky. Bald Mountain Basin smelled fresh, exciting, new, as we poked our swollen faces out of the tent, looked at each other, and kissed good morning – for it was a good morning. A decision to stay was made.*

Day 5: Pouring over the maps to reorganize our hike. No more climbing with huge packs. Roanne hadn't had a break in the last year and a half. After completing her three levels at the

Institute and spending the rest of her time working her tuition off as one of their head cooks, she drove cross-country to meet me in British Columbia and drive to Wyoming. The two of us may have started off on the wrong foot but were thankfully aware enough to change and restructure.

By this time the sun was overhead in a clear blue sky and with our revised plans and newborn attitude, a day hike to 11,600-foot Angel Pass was our goal. After climbing high on the southeastern crest of the basin I discovered, much to my surprise, that our campsite was not at Spider Lake but at one of the lower lakes. While up there, I picked out a provisional approach to the pass, then started a steep descent to the shoreline to find the route on our topo map, hopefully marked either by cairns or a worn footpath.

Roanne said she saw a person by the lake and I yelled and waved hoping to attract his attention so that I could ask about the fires. A father and his two sons were fishing. He pulled out a map and pointed to where the fires were, one under control and the other out. I recognized the map as the one that showed the first few miles of our first day, and asked if I could buy it from him after he said he didn't need it anymore. It was a friend's and he offered to loan it to us. I promised to mail it back to him and planned to meet the next day so that he could give us the map and his address. He also told us the time and Ro finally figured out how to set the clock on her camera.

Following the path plotted from the top of the ridge, Ro and I continued up a steep, bouldered incline, building cairns when the path disappeared so as not to get stuck on a ledge during our descent and left our backpack beside a rock close to the top. Finally scrambling over the last ridge into the vast rocky cradle of Angel Pass, I realized I was as high as I wanted to be. With clouds gathering at our backs and the top still a distance away, Roanne took the camera and continued. I watched her wend her way amidst smooth rock ledges, becoming smaller until she was a speck against a shocking blue sky. I heard her victory yell as she disappeared over the top, waited, scanning the heights, and suddenly spotted her on the way down. It took a half hour.

We proceeded to the spot where our pack had been left to perform a promised ritual for our friend Bonnie – to scatter some of her husband's ashes in the wilderness. Richard was one of our best friends and I felt grateful to be able to fulfill her request. I got ready to throw my half of the bag but broke down and had to wait for my tears to subside. After scattering his ashes, Roanne threw her half, very appropriately over an operatic outburst of "O Sole Mio." Richard was an opera buff. She and I spent a quiet moment before starting down.

At the lake while Roanne went swimming, I rinsed my hair in the icy water, then sat on the rocks eating apricots and almonds as a soft wind whispered and the sun's warmth

Ro and me at Angel Pass

wrapped around us, reminiscent of childhood days. It was fun, life was worth living and I felt less burdened.

Back at the tent we collapsed on our mats for a rest before dinner. Roanne dozed while I sketched the trees by our tent and read some Thoreau. Suddenly she awoke, looked over at me dreamily and said that somebody had just kissed her on the cheek. I smiled, knowing very well who it was – there was no doubt in my mind – an angel called Richard.

Trees outside our tent

Day 6: The sun warmed us while an arc of smoky grey cirrus clouds warned of fires far below. A man whistled for his dog as Ro and I enjoyed some *ume-sho-kuzu* tea she had prepared. A small white dog on the trail approached after Roanne gently coaxed him, cowered, and finally curled up close to our tent. He watched us eat breakfast, comfortable in his curiosity. It was pleasant to have a dog sit by our tent in the wilderness and Ro talked about getting one. I had never had a pet growing up because my mother was afraid of animals and I developed her fear, but promised myself that my kids would not inherit my untenable trait.

Coyotes cried in the distance and Roanne mimicked their howls, instigating them to continue. At 10:28 a.m. the first jet broke the sound barrier as the two of us roamed over smooth, amoebic rocks around the lower lakes. The jets continued at close intervals during lunch.

Suddenly a shout was heard from far-off. The fisherman and his boys had walked up to the basin to give us his map and address. He asked if we had a Chap Stick for his son's terribly chapped lips, and Roanne gave him one. When they heard the two of us were staying for two weeks, they inquired about our packhorses and were surprised that all our supplies had been carried on our backs. Out of earshot, Roanne quietly whinnied like a horse.

The skies were busy thoroughfares as the jets continued hauling humans to and fro across the continent. Oblivious to the momentum of the multitudes outside these wilderness walls, I was amazed one could climb into the backcountry and stop time, or slow it down enough to enjoy the minutes and hours that made up a day.

As I sat sketching the fire pit along the trail, the creek sang behind me, the birds called in the trees, the clouds sailed overhead, the sun shone intermittently, the wind shifted direction, and the jets continued. Fourteen planes so far. This was jet-counting day, confusing the illusion of where I was; six more jets over dinner, three as our dishes were washed and two more while doing yoga as the sun sank, leaving the Angel's wings etched against a slate sky. A slight smell of smoke drifted south from a fire that started a few days ago at Green River Lakes. While in bed playing gin rummy, four more jets passed.

Fire pit off Fremont Trail in Bald Mountain Basin

Day 7: At 8:00 a.m. the sky was clear. A tough night had found me up every couple of hours. The ground seemed harder than usual and our bodies were stiff and sore. It might be time to leave this idyllic spot. Over breakfast a route was examined into a side canyon where a lake tucked in a cirque beckoned us.

Climbing northwest of Spider Lake where blood-red rose crowns dotted patches of green amidst terraced smooth, amber and beige rock mounds, Ro and I walked along the west side of two large lakes, stepping on rocks that ringed the shoreline. Around a bend, the largest of the lakes nestled against the back of the canyon with what looked like a sandy beach.

After lunch – a bagel, carrot sticks, toasted almonds and dried apricots – we ran through the sand, our footprints dotting the beach where none were before and named Lake 10,950 Angel Beach. Short, sunny intervals and the sound of lapping water. A wonderful childhood memory came alive at that remote alpine lake on that August afternoon. I was seven years old, visiting my favorite aunt in Kennebunk, Maine. It was our yearly trip to the States for which I always awaited in anticipation. Fresh cooked lobsters, late night "color" television – there were only two black and white stations in Montreal – playing in the ocean, jumping waves, building sand castles and moats filled with water, delightful days frolicking on the beach.

Large billowing clouds rolled over the canyon walls hiding the sun's warmth, forcing us to leave. Reluctantly working our way back over the boulders, their dark-stained, exposed surfaces showing how low the water level was, a reality of global warming, Roanne exclaimed, "Look how far we have to come for privacy." Picked mertensia leaves for dinner greens while descending through sedimentary rocks coated with orange, red and yellow lichen. Between intermittent clouds, both of us washed in one of the lakes and dried in the sun's warmth. Dinner was enjoyed as the sun deserted the basin, leaving a stark, cold, clear landscape.

Day 8: A sliver of moon highlighted against brilliant blue cradled by Angel Pass was our first glimpse of the day. Reluctant to leave the world of dreams and soft, gentle sensations, the two of us dozed while wisps of translucent cloud spun a lacy web overhead and the sun brightened the hazy backdrop of the eastern sky. As it rose, clouds quilted around the peaks and reached for the rest of the sky while a slight breeze rustled the rainfly. The stillness closed in around us. I listened, thinking an animal was approaching, but it was only the beat of my heart. I realized it was the weekend and wondered what Marty was doing. The world beyond these mountains was hard-pressed to enter this one.

At 7:30 a.m. I went out to pee, took a moment to soak a cup of oats and diced apples, got back into my sleeping bag to savor the early morning hours and record my reflections. Roanne recounted her many dreams – feelings of invasion and indebtedness – and she talked about their likely origin: the divorce, the need to please, the inability to say no for fear of losing someone's – anyone's – love, and low self-esteem from having a father who had left her and a mother unable to come to grips with her adoption. Because of my low self-esteem, I felt at fault for everything that went on around me, which is how Roanne felt at the time of the divorce. She believed she was the cause of the separation and, at the time, I was so caught up in my own issues, I was not cognizant of hers.

Having been outside for eight days, I felt weathered – parched, burnt, strong, vibrant. I didn't experience my usual early morning stiffness and wondered if it was the yoga, my diet, or the vigorous outdoor living that kept my blood pumping at a different pace, feeding the tissues and carrying away the toxic elements of a sedentary life.

The first vaporous contrail appeared over Angel Pass and moments later the thunder of the jet's engines could be heard – passengers heading west to Salt Lake City and the coast for the Labor Day weekend – so much movement outside this plane of existence.

Living from moment to moment, aware of changes in weather, the need for clean water, warm food, warm clothing, the ability to alter well thought-out plans, made for a full-time occupation. Here the hours pass more slowly – doing nothing but strolling amidst the rocks and lakes of a ridged landscape, reading in a warm tent or drifting off into another dimension with a back-drop of chirping birds and a flutter of wings, a distant call of a hawk, the whisper of the wind around a canyon wall or the rainfly – all these pleasures reminded me that life was wonderful, that rest and relaxation were vital, and that simply keeping busy wasted our lives in accomplishing nothing of importance. Our reason for existence is all too often over-looked for a false sense of security promised by societal demands for accomplishment and the accumulation of things. We need so little and acquire so much and in the process miss the wonders of the natural world; the birds actually made music, the wind soothed a troubled brow, the sun warmed us, the moon moved our emotions, and the mountains' massive presence provided security which we strove for all our lives. Nature provides all if you're willing to take the risk.

I was still chilled after breakfast even though I was wearing my duofolds, turtleneck, down vest, sweater and wool hat. The clouds obscured the sun and Ro and I watched for a break. This isolated basin floating beneath a limitless sky was like a holding tank that lulled you into a semiconscious state of being.

Moving camp today, down three hundred feet to Cook Lakes, but first Roanne would try fishing at a lake somebody had told us about. Without any equipment a makeshift kit was assembled – a safety-pin bent into the shape of a hook, dental floss for a line, strips of silver paper from our veggie pack for a lure, a branch for a pole, and our plastic bag of mayflies Ro had been collecting for two days. She made a few attempts but the fish were smarter than we gave them credit for. With our eyes on the dark, threatening clouds that inflated my fear, she tried again half-heartedly and decided, at the first raindrops, to return to the tent, which was never close enough, to pack up and leave.

Our jackets were spread out to dry in the tent and the two of us settled in for a few hours under a soft, intermittent drizzle. *Ume- sho-kuzu* tea warmed our insides while gorging on bagels and tahini, awaiting a respite in the rain.

On our way down to Cook Lakes

There were still volumes of clouds tumbling into the basin. I took a last photograph of Angel Pass from a lower perspective and continued down the narrow, rocky path lined with tall, wet grass that dripped on my boots and through the weather-proofing. At the worn, wooden sign, Ro and I turned towards the lakes, reaching the creek and campsite we had enjoyed thirteen years earlier and settled into a familiar world.

Our tent went up, Ro soaked some quinoa and vegetables while I searched for a hanging tree – hard to find. Settling for a young spruce, she threw our weighted rope over the branches and when the rock hit the ground, pulled on both ends to see if the branch would hold our heavy bag. Dinner was delicious and, warmed by the sun, the two of us sat against a huge boulder sheltered from the wind and the few raindrops that fell. Our washed dishes were drying on that famous flat rock I had been looking at in the photograph from our 1987 trip. (page 60)

There were two large trees across Pole Creek and Roanne carefully crossed to the rocky islet, balancing easily. I shimmied

Campsite at Cook Lakes

across on my bottom rather ungracefully and as she and I explored the peninsula, the sun sank behind tattered clouds to the west of Mt. Lester. While talking on our rock, the lakes plunged into shadow, the sun dropped behind a darkened ridge, cloud bottoms turned red, and the lake was streaked with silver as fish bit for flies dimpling the glassy surface. Stayed until the alpenglow on the rocks faded and the valley turned grey and cold, about 9:00 p.m.

Day 9: In the morning I watched the clouds envelop the sky through the tent opening. The sun was already shining in the basin above but here in the trees, we'd have to wait. A mix of oatmeal and freeze-dried rice with broken walnuts made a fortifying breakfast while leaning against a fallen tree next to the murmuring brook.

Mid-morning found us on our way to Wall Lake. After a few undulating miles, this oblong, charcoal-blue body of water, ringed by sheer rock walls, appeared far below. Cairns were comforting as Ro and I followed a faint route around a steep outcropping that dropped quite suddenly to the water, a bit of an obstacle for me. The two of us finally descended to the flat, rocky ledges at the end of the lake where creeks from canyons off the Divide gathered to become the headwaters of Pole Creek.

A continuous cold wind sent us scurrying back to a sandy beach where Roanne tried in vain to get into the water but found the air too chilly. Luxuriating in our warm tent until dinner, a few hours were spent talking about leaving earlier than originally planned. Both of us loved the wilderness but there was always that pull to get out and join the rest of the world. To do what? Human beings have become human doings, having been brought up to do instead of to be. We decided to think about it tomorrow and to take each day at a time. Getting out our maps, she and I studied that ridge, searching how to stay high, counting the contours, trying to visualize the landscape, planning how to get down to our parked car. It would be a challenge.

A spectacular sunset sent me rushing for the camera to catch seven ducks in the lake flapping their feathers at the sky's brilliance. The clouds glowed red and gold against an aqua sky and stretched across the valley like pulled taffy into streams of tangerine, hot orange and blue. As soon as the colors faded, the air turned cold.

I was up at around 2:00 a.m. and had a difficult time falling back to sleep. The creek drowned all sound but I listened anyway for footsteps, having to remind myself that the outside didn't change during the night and all was well in the Winds. The time moved slowly and I must have dozed because it was bright when I next opened my eyes. Roanne had come to the decision not to leave early. I too was over the pressure, especially when awakening to a blue sky and the certainty of a sunrise.

Over breakfast a discussion about relationships came up about how some men put women down to build themselves up. Her boyfriend would question her about something, refute her answer only to find her right after somebody else confirmed what she said. It bothered her and she considered it a mild putdown. Marty sometimes did that to me. The fact that I allowed it to happen was the problem. Everybody has needs and seeking to fulfill them at somebody else's expense causes suffering.

The sun's rays illuminated my beautiful daughter's face as she lay next to me in her sleeping bag writing in her journal as I read my book. She remembered the sign for Gitchegumme on her travels through Canada and said she would love to see eastern Canada, especially Prince Edward Island. I told her about my travels in the Maritimes – Cape Breton Highlands, the Cabot Trail, Glace Bay, Sydney and about an affair I had had. She was getting to know all my secrets, so perhaps, in turnabout, her skeletons could come out of the closet too. I felt relieved at unburdening myself to her, secure in the fact that she would not be accusing or denigrating, that she would understand my dilemmas, what led me to do the things I did. She needed to know all about me.

My palms were stained and fingernails blackened with the dirt of the outdoors. Soap was left at home because just rinsing in the lakes kept us clean. Perhaps the grime of the city required more frequent cleansing but out here the living was different. The wind didn't seem laden with toxins, the rain rinsed the dirt off our skin, the sun kept our bodies at a healthy temperature and our sweat was carried off by the breeze.

While walking behind Roanne yesterday, I noticed her shapely, youthful legs with skin so taut, as opposed to mine which didn't hold up as well anymore. Neither did I. Walking in the wilderness had kept me young, able to carry a load, secure in the knowledge I had gleaned from years of outdoor life, with a willingness to take risks and make quick changes. Memories from all my trips were as clear now as they ever were and I felt fortunate to continue to find freedom in a world that has taken it away from so many. I should say rather that we have given up our freedom to those who would take it away. Without our independence we were nothing and our lives were spent answering not our own hearts, nor fulfilling our own needs, but those of others.

At 12:30 p.m. Ro and I headed for the sandy beach at Upper Cook Lake. She went in for a quick swim and came out just before another cloud passed, bringing a cold wind. While lounging by the lake eating lunch, a couple suddenly emerged

Upper Cook Lake

from the woods looking for the Fremont Trail, unaware that they were heading the wrong way. How they got this far off the trail was puzzling, although it has certainly happened to us, and I pointed them in the right direction. Off they went unconcerned.

After two hours of easy hiking around the lakes, the infamous and sometimes treacherous Pole Creek Crossing – deep and wide – separated us from our campsite. Searching for the shallowest spot after hanging our boots from our packs, the rushing creek was conquered.

Back at our tent I talked about how disappointed I was that, after twenty-seven years of living together and finally getting married, none of my daughters or friends had acknowledged my marriage to Marty. Not that I expected gifts or cards, but some gesture of acceptance would have been nice from my children. My granddaughter was the only one who enjoyed the idea of the marriage by planning a party for us visiting her in British Columbia. Feeling guilty, Roanne kept asking if Marty and I were disappointed in her. I didn't want to hurt her feelings, knowing she would never purposely do anything to upset us. I hadn't planned on saying anything, but it had been on my mind, and this was how I had to get to it, through the back door; I should have been more straightforward.

Roanne said she needed to know, that there shouldn't be any secrets between us, and if I didn't tell her she would end up making something up on her own, probably worse. She was

right, of course. Tears came to my eyes because I felt inadequate
as a mother, not being able to level with my daughter. I worried
about her love and she reassured me that she loved me more
than anything else in the world. She hated to think Marty and I
might talk about her behind her back and needed to know our
feelings up front. Why was I afraid to be honest?

It takes courage to voice your feelings and I didn't always
have it. That old enemy, rejection, paralyzed me and my capacity
to be candid vanished. I had been brought up to hide my true
sentiments and had a difficult time expressing myself for fear of
being given away. I grew up with the anxiety of abandonment.

Over dinner she and I talked more about our dilemma. It
became easier for me to discuss this problem and our acute
emotions subsided. After chores the two of us climbed into our
sleeping bags, exhausted, both physically and emotionally.
Tomorrow a move down to Chain Lakes on our way back to
civilization.

Day 10: When I opened my eyes in the morning Roanne's
smiling face, upside-down outside the tent opening, made me

Arnica

smile and the day began. After breakfast I sketched the flowers
by the log I was leaning against, while Roanne wrote in her
journal. The wind picked up as she attempted to go swimming,
and she and I ended up sitting on some rocks staring across the
rippled lake into the far mountains. I don't know how long we

stayed there but lunch was overlooked and because of the chill in the air, a decision to pack up and depart for lower elevations was made.

The Cook Lakes Trail joined the Highline Trail heading to Pole Creek Lakes where Ro and I would be encountering hikers coming in from Elkhart Park, but it didn't bother us having been alone for so long. Moving mainly through a forest of pine and spruce, a climb up an arduous ridge brought us down to three formidable creek crossings and eventually into a large horse camp where there were two tents and a few people milling about. Heading southwest to Chain Lakes I realized that Ro and I had circled Mt. Baldy. Too exhausted to search for a suitable site in this narrow valley with a creek running through the middle, and mindful of the fact that camping within one hundred feet of water is prohibited, I remembered having seen that yellow tent on the way in and walked to the only campsite in the area, now understanding why those hikers had chosen that spot. Too worn out to eat all of our dinner, the leftovers were placed in the bag that had held the freeze-dried pasta and sealed tightly, hoping the smell wouldn't permeate the bag, and hung it far away from our tent. After filtering water the two of us sat on a rock and watched the clouds turn silver, blue and pastel yellow and finally fade to smoky grey as the sun dropped behind the ridge.

Roanne seemed distant, and, when I asked about her moodiness, said she felt totally introverted having written in her journal so much yesterday. She called me crabby and I agreed with her. Living in such close quarters, it was important to communicate and not close down. I started to read by flashlight, feeling indulgent about using the batteries being at the end of our trip. She asked if I'd like to play cards and lit a candle and resorted to the use of the flashlight as well while playing four games of gin rummy, all of which she won.

She brought up the fact that she had decided not to stay with her boyfriend if he didn't try to work at curing himself, and she and I talked about why some people can cure themselves while others can't. Maybe with her support, something he never had from his family who knew nothing of his condition, his energy and will to survive would be enhanced. I guess that had been on her mind, enough to make her melancholy.

Day 11: It was raining lightly at 7:00 a.m. Two hours later Roanne retrieved our food bag under a low grey ceiling that didn't look like it would lift. The two of us sat cross-legged in the tent catching up on our journals. Intermittent rain diminished to a drizzle and by noon it finally stopped, giving us time to pack.

The landscape, muted in medium grays, and the grasses, glowed orange and yellow while hiking towards Barnes Lake – two miles on a muddy trail. My boots got wet instantly, so much for the waterproofing, but my duofolds under a turtle-neck, down vest, sweater and poncho preserved the warmth generated by a hearty breakfast. The Timico Lake Trail took off from the Highline which continued south, and suddenly, around a bend, a huge bull moose, not more than twenty-five feet away, scared Roanne who was ahead of me. He started towards us and just as she and I were about to run for a tree, abruptly turned and took off into the forest. Talking loudly, we hastened past him, checking back to make sure there was enough distance between us.

The sign for Lake Jacqueline appeared and since it was too early in the day to stop, Ro and I continued to Belford Lake, wanting to get as close as possible to that illusive trail which would hopefully take us to our car.

Climbing a craggy hill, a rocky plateau was quietly crossed as the mist, eerie and ghostlike, enveloped us, muting all sound and color. Leaving this shrouded, surreal highland and entering the trees, the remnants of Black's cabins at the lake came into view. Finally lowering our packs onto the only dry spot under a tree, the last of the rice cakes and tahini were devoured as raindrops pooled around us.

Settling on a site, the wet pine needles were cleared and the tent erected under a light drizzle. Hot tea warmed us and I knew we were in for a long, damp, cold night. When the rain stopped, Ro and I, anxious to locate the cairn left on our way in, hiked up the trail that, if lucky, would lead us to the correct trail to our car rather than the bushwhacking we did on our way in. Just past the cairn Roanne came upon a well-worn path that disappeared into the woods and, following it for a while, decided it must be the one. Back at the tent just in time for the next deluge the two of us were happy with the promise of being able to retrace our route.

After dinner she built a fire to burn our trash, feeling it was safe because it was wet everywhere. While luxuriating in its warmth, voices were heard and thinking somebody had seen the smoke, hurriedly doused it with dirt only to find two hikers on their way to Cook Lakes. Their friend had forgotten his sleeping bag in Jackson, gone back to get it, and would be four and a half hours behind them. They set up their tent in the remains of one of the cabins and I was sure their friend would see ours first and think it was theirs. As the rain started again Ro and I climbed into our tent and played four games of gin rummy with candles lit and flashlight on, throwing all caution to the wind; dry and warm and excited about tomorrow.

It was around midnight when I heard footsteps and whistling and suddenly a flashlight pierced the night. I called out that this was the wrong tent and was immediately plunged into darkness. The whistling kept on until it started to fade in the distance and I realized that he had missed his friends' tent and walked on. I yelled again and again until one of them woke and went after him. When they returned, they were noisy for a long time.

Day 12: It rained throughout the night and when I went to get the food bag, I was shocked to see how soaked the ground was. While Ro made tea, I planned our getaway, resigned to the fact that from the time both of us stepped out of the tent, we would be wet for the rest of the day. Reluctantly, our damp cold boots were pulled on over dry warm socks, our stuff was lined up at the doorway and we went for it. I handed the packs to her and she placed them on her foam pad under a tree to keep dry; the tent was dismantled and stuffed into its sack; the site was surveyed making sure nothing was left and Roanne and I headed up the trail past the other tent sitting in a pool of water.

The trail was muddy, visibility poor. Sliding and sinking into puddles, our boots filled with water while climbing past our cairn to the unmarked path and turned west into the fogbound forest, an alien land of fallen trees, thick underbrush and faint trails. Every time the trail vanished, she and I split up and searched. My heart picked up when I heard Roanne yell, "I got it" from the other side of a wooded hillock. Our eyes strained to pick out Burnt Lake below, but the fog was impenetrable. Down we went for hours, the trail at times well defined or divided into parallel tracks, at others, just a slight depression. Wandering around fallen logs, under bent branches of gnarled tree trunks, through scrub brush, knowing only to stay high and head west.

Finally a recognizable grassy opening appeared. Suddenly Roanne remembered a creek crossing, then the log on which she and I stopped to rest and finally the long ridge where we had lost our way. Relief mixed with joy. Even the rain had stopped. The meadow where the cows had congregated gradually became visible through the cloud cover. After three and a half uneasy hours, we were back.

A strange feeling came over me that I hadn't been anywhere and the whole trip was a dream. For a fleeting moment I felt disorientated. Walking, walking, walking for so many miles, so much emotion, such grandeur, so difficult to come down and be here now.

I couldn't contain my excitement when, rounding a bend, I saw our car just as it had been left almost two weeks ago. Euphoric, our packs dropped to the ground for the last time, off with our boots, socks peeled from damp skin, and Roanne retrieved the car key so carefully guarded for so long. Just before changing into dry clothing she joined me in a last photograph. As I drove the long, ten miles over the rutted, rocky road, washed away in spots, she smothered our rice cakes, left in the car for just this moment, with the bit of tahini we had managed to save, and finished the last almonds and apricots. On the highway I felt removed and had to deliberately concentrate on the driving because I wasn't used to moving through space so quickly.

Roanne drove the rest of the way to Jackson after stopping to call Marty to tell him she and I were out and safe. It was over for another year until the next trip when the two of us would do it all again.

Me and Ro

Roanne's journal: *She broke down*
in the middle of the night
She wanted out
had second sight
tears of guilt
that burned those cheeks
burst and fell
soaking the quiet night
Behind this waterfall
A relic worn down
grief stricken
so beautiful
blazened with grey and black
This steadfast earth-ship;
A mother
her own rig to grip
satin smooth she goes
clutching vestiges
of tissues
in piles they form
soggy from the storm...
half moon rises,
she lies inside
desperate for her
home to reach
desperate for the
dark to cease.

"Walking is the true speed of the soul and . . . when we travel too fast, in cars and planes, we separate from our soul." Derek W. Youngs

XVI

First Hike of the Season

The creek alongside our cabin in Canada opened on April 19th, a whisper of spring; sold our Calgary house and moved our stuff into the cabin and then to Daniel, Wyoming where we had purchased a homestead on thirteen acres with a view of the Wind Rivers.

July 2001:

It was 11:25 a.m. when Roanne and I started the long drive from our cabin in Daniel to the Big Sandy Opening. Living so close to the Winds allowed us the luxury of sleeping in and leaving later in the morning. The parking lot was full but finally a space in the grass in full sun was found.

There were scattered clouds at the start of the six-mile hike through the forest to the lake. In less than a mile the wilderness boundary was crossed and I felt the way I always do in the backcountry – free, independent, relaxed and happy. Why does wilderness do this for me? Is my life so cumbersome? Do we all live lives of quiet desperation denying that we do? Is everything out of our control? Do we have the power to change anything?

I walk and my thoughts find their way to areas I don't seem to go to while at home. Summer is so short on the high desert and it is always well into July before the mountains allow entrance to their snowy domains.

The trail, lined with arnica, bluebells and monkeyflowers was clear and dry. A few hikers passed and wondered where we were headed. Our lunch of nori rolls beside a creek near clumps of Parry's primrose allowed Sachi, Roanne's dog, time to get wet and excited. This was our first hike accompanied by a four-footed friend.

It had been thirteen years since we were on this trail, that time with Karen (page 67), heading for the Cirque of the Towers. Nothing seemed familiar until our arrival at Big Sandy Lake where I recognized the turn towards Jackass Pass and the Cirque at its northwest corner. And there in the distance loomed mile-long Haystack Mountain that I had been staring at for years in my hiking book.

Three parallel valleys drained into Big Sandy Lake; the one closest to the Divide housed Black Joe Lake; the middle, Deep and Clear Lakes, where Ro and I were headed; and the last, Temple, Miller and Rapid Lakes with Temple Peak, the second highest peak in the southern Winds, at its head. Continuing around the north shore picking up the Little Sandy Trail that led east through an open meadow, Black Joe Creek was crossed, and, about a half mile later, the trail leading up to that lake. Proceeding along the swampy edge of the meadow, a turn to the east at a poorly marked junction led to the steep mile through thin forest to our destination, Clear Lake, a high basin bound by granite monoliths, 11,978-foot Haystack Mountain and 12,590-foot East Temple Peak to the east, 11,624-foot Schiestler Mountain and 12,972-foot Temple Peak to the west.

There were no empty campsites around the lake; passed a few tents and continued on through shrub willow, up sloping polished bedrock slabs, across the lake's inlet and, a ways upstream the two of us stumbled upon an ideal spot in some trees at the foot of Haystack Mountain. At 4:15 p.m. our tent was up, food hung, and while Roanne and Sachi slept, I listened to a light drizzle, happy to be where I was. I couldn't believe that I had never heard of this valley, one of the most beautiful places in the Winds.

Day 2: After breakfast, the three of us played on smooth rock amidst meandering streams. I sketched the mountain and photo-graphed a clump of Parry's primroses beside a rock in the lake.

The magnificent magenta color of the petals and brilliant green foliage were electrifying. After lunch Ro, Sachi and I left for the mile hike up to Deep Lake nestled against East Temple Peak. Looking back I could see Pingora in the Cirque of the Towers.

Roanne and Sachi in the Rapid Lake Valley with the Cirque in the distance

After climbing west over a low divide to Temple Lake, we stashed our packs, pinning them down with heavy rocks because of the wind, and turned south for the 1.2-mile climb to Temple Pass to see what lay beyond. This pass was used by Indians on horseback, but because of rockslides it is practical only for foot travel now.

It was tough going and I stopped to rest, telling Roanne to continue without me. Soon after she left, I started up again and met her at the top. Nothing profound on the other side and, descending to the lake, retrieved our packs and continued down to Miller and finally Rapid Lake where the two of us searched for a site.

A NOLS group was scattered amongst the sculptured limber pines but a private niche was found, our tent went up in just enough time for a walk down to the lake to enjoy the last rays of the setting sun. After dinner we did it again and just kicked around, throwing twigs into the water for Sachi to retrieve.

The sky was clear, no wind and I hoped this would be a quiet night. Suddenly a dark shape hurtled by our tent opening and disappeared into the trees on the far side. A bear. It couldn't have been anything else – too big to be a small animal and too small to be a really big animal.

Day 3: A clear day dawned. After breakfast as the sun rose high above East Temple, I sketched one of the limber pines and took some photos of Ro and Sachi curled up in its trunk. A few hours later after packing up and searching for the Rapid Creek Trail, the three of us started the long descent to Big Sandy Lake and the closing of our loop. It was surprising to see the number of hikers with dogs. I don't ever remember seeing so many dogs with packs on before. Perhaps since Sachi had joined us, I was more aware of it. Our first hike of the season into new territory was stimulating. Where to next?

XVII

Back to Bonneville

August 2001:

At 6:40 a.m. the sun rose over the north end of Mt. Bonneville. It had been a difficult walk from the Scab Creek trailhead. Roanne and I didn't talk – just walked. There were a lot of people, packhorses and hikers coming out. I was surprised to see so much traffic on this strenuous trail.

I thought we were at Divide Lake (the half-way point) when stopping for lunch on a rock at a marshy pond but we weren't even close. Scattered clouds. Ro and I had tried to get to the Bonneville Lakes nine years ago in 1992 and, realizing that more time was needed to do them justice, had promised to return.

As I walked I thought about Karen and our lack of communication; about Maxine and our superficial relationship; about the reality of never knowing who my real mother is and having no delusions of ever meeting her. Although, at times, I catch myself daydreaming about the feelings I would have if such a scenario came about.

The last mile to Dream Lake seemed to go on forever and the two of us were beat when our old campsite materialized. It was all familiar. This place stays the same while we change. Or at least our lives change quite constantly and quickly compared to the slow changes of nature. It's as if I returned to find I had never left.

"The landscape, by its patient resting there, teaches me that all good remains with him that waiteth." Henry David Thoreau

Our new MSR Whisperlite stove worked well; no more disposable canisters. Dinner: a salty quinoa stew with carrots, corn and greens, bread and tahini and chamomile tea while the clouds dispersed and finally disappeared. No wind. A perfect evening. It was dark at 9:30 p.m. except for an almost full moon lighting up a clear sky. Suddenly, voices and laughter from people arriving late, not close enough to be intrusive; the bleating of sheep and yelps of coyote in the distance. Otherwise quiet.

Roanne reminded me of the time I had made the decision to leave this spot because of a blizzard. She had wanted to stay. So did I and felt burdened by cutting our trip short. She wasn't happy about it either.

Up almost every hour. I wasn't anxious about not sleeping through the night and felt rested as if I had. It's interesting to stay awake, to just be there, hear the sounds and experience the night as we do the day. The hours pass slowly. You can hear the breath of the universe – long soft sighs. The breezes pick up and die; no refrigerator hum, no clock ticking, no fan whirring, no heat pump recycling, no computer/modem lights, no cell phone glow. Nothing.

Sachi slept at my head. It was comforting to hear her even breathing and her unconcern of any potential intrusion. She teaches Roanne patience and makes her laugh a lot.

We discovered that it was more important for us to face east and the early morning sun rather than being in the shadow of the mountains facing west and an evening sunset – always a dilemma when choosing a site. This is such a spacious basin with so few people, never more than two tents, that one can still experience wilderness in the Winds.

Day 2: Bonneville Basin with over sixty lakes was our destination. We started out as soon as the breakfast dishes were done, our food hung, and my smaller backpack packed with everything needed for the day ahead. Crossing the mile-long meadow to Raid Lake took no time. (Named as such to pay tribute to a 1903 sheep massacre. Increasing conflict between ranchers over grazing rights had reached a highpoint that summer and cattlemen slaughtered over 1,200 animals – talk about the Wild West!) Turning east along the South Fork of Boulder Creek, an unmarked trail was followed between the grassy slopes of the Pronghorn-Dragonhead and Raid-Geikie ridges. Sunlit moss on whitebark pine.

Little Bonneville Lake at 10,521 feet – smooth rocks across its middle and a shortcut was attempted. The water was deep and crossing from one rock to another, I suddenly slipped and slid effortlessly into the cold lake. I couldn't believe I was waist-deep in water and just stood there, bewildered. Roanne couldn't believe it either and casually reached over and pulled me out. She looked at me, worried. "I never saw you do that, Ma," she murmured. This was a first. Sixty-one – perhaps the beginning of my senior years of backpacking when things start to happen. I thought I'd never grow old and never stop hiking. Lucky the day was so hot.

The trail followed the west shore to a 300-foot, steep cliff and Bonneville Lake, a large, rockbound, shimmering body of water at the foot of 12,585-foot, mile-long Bonneville Mountain just off the Divide. It was one of those hand-grabbing, knee-bumping ascents where whatever is behind is not there anymore and what's up ahead is too high and steep to get to. How was I going to negotiate the descent?

Lunch while sitting on a smooth rock that gradually submerged into the water and eventually disappeared into its depths; luxuriating in the warmth and windless heights while Sachi roamed the rocks and stunted brush.

Roanne had awakened this morning with a scratchy throat which meant she needed to talk about something rather than internalize it. One of her friends puts her down and she is not able to stand up for herself -- so like her mother. Not wanting to upset the apple cart, she, in the end, is the one who suffers.

A decision was made to turn back after boulder-hopping around the lake towards the north end of the canyon because Roanne wanted to go swimming down below and, as she well knew, her mother was worried about the threatening precipitous descent ahead.

Instead of backtracking the two of us headed for the waterfall to see if that would be easier. She climbed down first and when she called for me to follow, I carefully picked my way over the slippery boulders surrounded by rushing water and crisscrossed the steep rocky incline. Sachi, pacing back and forth across the top of the falls, barked and yelped and I knew she felt like I did about the dangerous drop-off. Roanne said she would follow but she wasn't moving. I continued down and rounded a rocky outcrop where Roanne reappeared. She called up to Sachi. We waited. "Come on, Ma, she'll come." But she didn't. Continuing on, she finally disappeared from our view. Roanne called to her again and again and upon reaching safe ground, had to climb back to get her. She couldn't believe it, like she couldn't believe the sight of me sliding into the lake.

Back at Little Bonneville Lake an alcove out of the wind materialized under scattered clouds in a very blue sky. Sachi leapt into the freezing water while her posed, naked mistress dove in and swam around until her body gradually reached a bearable temperature. Sachi didn't last long, and, wet and scrawny-looking, dug a hollow in the wet earth behind me and settled in securely.

Suddenly a few hikers appeared in the distance. They slowly moved around the lake, diminishing in size as they continued towards the falls and finally disappeared into the vastness of the basin. After packing up, Ro and I climbed a hill to get a last look at the environs and talked about hiking over the west ridge of Bonneville into the adjacent deep valley of the upper East Fork. The gradual, grassy west slopes would bring us into view of the steep east faces of the Raid, Ambush and Geikie Peaks. Deciding that there wasn't enough time before dark, we started down through the trees and finally emerged into the great Bonneville Basin housing Raid and Dream Lakes. The tent was a welcome sight after a long day.

A still night allowed us the luxury of a fire while watching the sky darken and stars appear. Suddenly a slight wind brushed the flames and Ro doused them quickly, afraid of a spark catching a dry blade of grass. Our water was used up to put out the fire. It was after 10:00 p.m. when the two of us climbed into our bags and made Sachi comfortable. Roanne's throat was back to normal. Talking, unloading, dealing with it, usually does the trick.

With two days before the full moon I was up every few hours. The tent was light and when the moon rose, it was as if a street light was turned on.

Day 3: At 6:00 a.m. Sachi accompanied me when I went out to answer the call of nature. Roanne decided to get up and filter water. The sun was hot, a few quilted clouds stretched above the peaks to the northeast of the Divide and a discussion ensued about where to go next. Living so close now makes the mountains available and before one trip is over, plans for the next are in the making. The hike out was long and relentless and a promise was made not to ever use this trailhead again. It's just too damn difficult. We also didn't get the same comfortable feeling as before at Dream Lake and couldn't figure out why.

XVIII

Indian Pass

August 2001:

Almost three weeks later, on August 25, Elkhart Park, the easiest access into the range, was our choice, not ever wanting to do Scab Creek again. Halfway to Seneca Lake, our first campsite, a guy sitting alongside the trail with a bum knee warned us about a big black bear around Lost Lake, just down from Seneca. My suggestion, of course, was to try and make Island Lake, fifteen miles, to avoid the bear, but Roanne thought it was too far. Seneca was perfect, nine miles.

Having always had a problem finding a campsite here, this time was no different. The two of us ended up passing both Seneca and Little Seneca Lakes and kept walking until, unexpectedly, Island Lake appeared over a rise. Too exhausted to continue looking for a site, a dusty, dry spot close to the lake, which was extremely low, was settled on. There were people close by and a couple just above us in the trees.

It wasn't as I had remembered – a lot more compact, not as broad an area as Dream Lake; the jumping-off point for Titcomb Basin and all lakes to the north and, like Big Sandy in the south, always busy. Both of us were up almost every hour during the night being in such close proximity to people, although it was quiet and still.

Day 2: The sun was high in the sky but because the tent was in the shadow of the forested hillside it remained cold. I wanted to change sites, Roanne wasn't sure. When the chance arose to move after the couple above had left, everything was dumped into the center of the tent and dragged up the ridge to a tiny, treed area where the sun was shining and you could see the entire valley. As I put my boots on and started out, my left Achilles tendon was quite sore and I loosened the lacing leaving the top open. I had had this feeling after our last trip and thought there might be something wrong with my new boots.

10:30 a.m., Ro and I passed a couple with two llamas and their guide in a meadow by the lake. I read somewhere that Indian Pass was two miles beyond the Titcomb Lakes cutoff but the signpost read six miles. Roanne was surprised and a bit impatient, questioning me as to where I had read that. I felt guilty having made such an error. I don't normally. But, as she said, we had all day and the weather was great and so what.

Turning east the two of us climbed into rocky, desolate Indian Basin, surrounded by Fremont Peak, Jackson Peak, Knife Point Mountain and Harrower (Ellingwood) Peak, all over 13,000 feet. There were strange feelings between us because I had asked to see her infected finger that she had complained about the day before and she got crazy. I don't like to be in the wilderness with anything physically wrong and was worried when her finger had blown up. Thinking it would go away, she took no precautions. I guess she didn't like being treated like a child and rebelled. Continuing to climb into the surreal surroundings, she finally relaxed.

I wondered if being together was getting old, if hiking has become a habit? Habits are difficult to break. The desire to get into the mountains, not able to go alone and not knowing anybody else to go with, we are rather stuck with one another. Perhaps each of us has issues to deal with at this time and being apart would be beneficial. It would be good to talk about this.

The going was easy, the route well marked, and one cannot be angry for long amidst such beauty. Filled our water bottles with spring water coming from some high rocks and continued on, climbing between Jackson Peak and Knife Point Mountain. The glaciers were beautiful, the day, a scorcher, and she and I covered up to keep from getting too sunburnt.

Up through the rocks, along grassy ledges the two of us continued to the top of 12,120-foot Indian Pass – the main route over the Divide before the coming of the white man – with a remarkable view of the Brown Cliffs on the other side. We chose the only shady spot to sit down and rest, and the moment our packs hit the ground, a guy walked up, remarked about our site and dropped his pack right next to ours. After climbing six miles to the Divide to be alone and enjoy the view and find company? Weird. We moved into the sun and settled on a rock for some lunch. The guy approached Sachi trying to make friends but Sachi growled at him, something she rarely does. He then appeared next to us in an attempt to scrape some ice from the glacier's edge into his water bottle. Both of us felt awkward and after lunch returned to the other side, found a rock with a view and relaxed in the sun for about an hour, feasting on some dried apricots and the landscape.

Started down slowly, not wanting to lose altitude too quickly, and stopped often. Roanne had decided she wanted to learn how to whistle in order to get Sachi to come. She curled her lips around her thumb and third finger and commenced to blow. It took a while for a squeak to come out. She tried again and again and sometimes it was loud enough for Sachi to turn and eventually saunter over.

Suddenly, I tripped and fell onto my knees and right wrist. The pain was so intense I couldn't catch my breath. Roanne told me to cry, to get it out, and finally the tears came. I moaned until the pain subsided, limped down to a small pool, and knelt in the frigid water to soothe the bruises that were quickly becoming quite swollen. Roanne submerged but surfaced immediately because of the cold.

Not one prone to accidents when hiking, I must have been pre-occupied with the incident on the Divide. It probably bothered me more deeply than I thought, reminding me of my inability to express my feelings. I should have told the guy to get lost.

Back to the tent at 7:00 p.m. and cooked dinner. I strapped my knee with an ace bandage because the pressure on my kneecap was too painful when turning over in my sleeping bag and worried about the fifteen-mile hike out tomorrow.

Day 3: The temperature had plunged during the night and Sachi's water bowl was frozen. Another beautiful blue day. My knee was stiff and sore, the kneecap very swollen. Some hot tea with granola warmed us while waiting for the barley flakes to cook.

By 10:00 a.m. we were on the trail. My physiotherapy training came in handy as I worked on changing the pattern of my gait: walking downhill my sore right leg was first to step down. That way it could remain straight; uphill, my left leg took the lead so I didn't have to bend my right knee. Roanne found a stick and padded the top with some foam, tying it on with my neckerchief. It worked well, allowing me to take some weight off my right leg. Proficiency was mastered within three miles and walking was less laborious.

I kept looking back at Indian Pass, now a familiar landmark. The Shoshone and Absarokas (Crow) had found that pass through the mountains easy enough for their horses.

A stop at Seneca Lake provided a cool dip for Sachi and some roasted pumpkin seeds for us. Up and down to Hobbs and Barbara Lakes, deciding to wait until Photographers Point for lunch. Clouds had collected around the peaks, especially over Fremont and Jackson where the sky had been blue just hours before. Heading into more clouds and rain seemed likely.

The couple with the llamas and guide seen the day before stopped to chat. They were from upstate New York and traveling cross country, hitting the high peaks in the West. When they heard where we lived, they said they preferred the East because of the Jewish community and camaraderie back there. Their guide worked for a climbing outfit in Jackson and part-time for Harrison Ford who gave him a lot of clothes. Lucky boy!

By now the path had become less rocky, wider and easier for me. They eventually caught up with us and we talked for about a mile's worth. He was a professional engineer who did radio frequency and EMF exposure assessments and was interested when I talked about radionics and how they affected our health. She was an artist and teacher. Roanne became impatient with me for talking so much and falling back and, feeling guilty, I rushed to keep up with her. But I was enjoying myself. I liked to hear about people, where they were from, what they did, why they came here to hike and where they've been.

Arriving at our car at 6:00 p.m., the sky having cleared somewhat, I was grateful to get off my leg. The New York gentleman gave me his card and if we were ever to come east, to call.

Perhaps a change is in the offing. This trip was strange, both of us feeling a bit misplaced. Never did get to talk about our hiking habits. Our need to get into the wilderness was a fact understood. Perhaps our lives were in flux and we had to move on. The change would be gradual – always difficult but unavoidable. Our approach would be different. But the wilderness would always be there for us.

The Universe has a way of warning about change – if we listen. The flow of life becomes strained. Things are not as easy as they used to be. When things happen easily, it's meant to be. Our path is clear. The channels are open. There are no obstacles.

And I realized, after some time, that another boundary was being crossed: that of age, endurance, my daughter pursuing her own life independent of mine; and a sudden twisting in my gut assures me of the veracity of my feelings.

"There is a tide in the affairs of men;
Which if taken at flood leads to fortune.
Omitted, all the voyage of their life
Is bound in shallows and miseries."

William Shakespeare

XIX

Summit Lake

September 2001:
A week later Marty dropped us at the Elkhart Park entrance
again at 10:15 a.m. Normally we come out at the same trailhead
but this time, rather than a loop, a one-way trip had been
planned. Last night Roanne's car was left at the New Fork Lakes
trailhead, our destination.

Day 1: My knee was better. I had been working on it for a
week, doing hot and cold compresses four times a day, and the
swelling was down – just the kneecap was sensitive to the touch.
After strapping it and checking our packs, the two of us were on
our way. Lunch at Seneca Lake gave Sachi time to play in the
water. My leg was tired after seven hours of walking and I just
barely made the last two hills to Island Lake.

Much to our dismay our usual spot was occupied. A couple
with two llamas and three dogs had set up their tent in the shade
and arranged their kitchen in the next site – a bit extravagant for
one party to take up two campsites and I asked the couple who
were with them and camping above us if they were definitely
going to stay there. As he looked over to the woman in her
kitchen, she motioned, very definitely – they were not moving.
People sure like to spread their stuff around, totally oblivious of
their surroundings. Island Lake was a busy area and a tight spot
for camping. It is amazing how selfishly unaware people can be
even in the wilderness.

There were tents all over the place and a sandy spot
surrounded by trees was finally settled on, knowing that if it
rained our tent would probably end up in a mud puddle and

would be difficult keeping the inside clean. The other couple whom I had spoken to walked through our site with their dogs and, of course, Sachi rose to the occasion. She growled and barked and Roanne got crazy.

Having seen a tent high up on a knoll on the other side of the lake when last here, Ro and I checked it out and found too much horse manure to camp there. Too tired to keep searching, having already walked fifteen miles and another one around the lake . . . I guess she and I couldn't always have the wilderness to ourselves. The thought of crossing Island Lake off our list was becoming likely.

Dinner in the shelter and privacy of a clump of trees was enjoyed despite the llama people walking back and forth from their kitchen to their sleeping area and the other couple walking back and forth with their dogs. Two guys who had erected their tent up above near a well-marked "sensitive area" were quite loud and came down to take a picture of the llamas. I thought of asking them to pipe down but was too exhausted to climb up to their spot and confront them.

The sunset calmed our unsettled souls while watching the red and gold in the west, the alpenglow on Fremont and Jackson Peaks in the east and Elephant Head behind us; a dark, rich crimson slowly faded to maroon and cocoa brown. After doing some stretches, we climbed into the tent at 8:30 p.m. while everybody was still out and about. The guys were loud which made us angry. Sachi, exhausted, curled up on her blanket at the head of the tent and slept deeply. Talked for a few hours as it drizzled intermittently, so calming to our stressful situation; awake for much of the night.

Day 2: It was cloudy at 6:30 a.m. and the guys started talking again. My anger was rising and at 7:30 a.m. when Roanne and Sachi went out to pee, I got dressed, walked up to their tent and asked them to please drop their voices. One of them apologized saying he sometimes forgot that he wasn't alone up here.

Tea warmed us while waiting for our cereal to cook. It drizzled lightly. Although comfortable the two of us talked about whether to move or stay put. The people congregated in their kitchen area. The other couple was staying. The guys were leaving. Not wanting to carry our packs every day our decision was made to remain in our spot. It was 9:30 a.m.

Titcomb Basin didn't seem as spacious as I had remembered. Wandered over the boulder-strewn valley until clouds moved in and it started to rain. At the second lake the sun suddenly appeared, brightening the valley and our spirits in time for lunch. Spreading our ponchos out to dry on the smooth rocks around us Ro and I sat quietly, staring at the peaks. Sachi ran loose until a hiker appeared in the distance. Clouds appeared again and the rain, thunder and lightning sent us scurrying for shelter beside a huge boulder. Sachi climbed under Roanne's poncho. She was shaking pretty badly and Roanne held her close. Storms like this always make me wonder why I am where I am, and I am so happy to survive them.

We took an alternate route back to Island Lake and arrived at our tent, wet and tired. Some grain coffee while sitting outside in our treed kitchen hit the spot. A full pot of pasta and vegetables followed as the sun came out.

At sunset in an almost clear blue sky I noticed an opaque blue shape that resembled a mountain ridge in the distance. I remembered the western horizon to be flat. A little later when focusing on the edge of the world, I realized that a heavy bank of clouds had collected with no break or blue beyond. It didn't look good. But it was far off and I didn't want to think about it. After awhile I changed focus from the brilliant sunset to that dense cardboard cloud cutout which was becoming more predominant and finally mentioned it to Roanne who had seen it as well and didn't want to bring it up.

Dozed on and off and at 10:00 p.m. Roanne asked about the lightning. Was I aware of it? I was. And then that far-off, undeniable rumbling. Both of us knew what was inevitable.

It was the storm of all storms where you lie in your tent and wait, not speaking. Thunder ripped through the valley, tearing around the peaks, and the lightning sparked my nervous system and tweaked my muscles into trembling. The thunder crashed just seconds after the flashes and we waited for the blast. Rain pelted down on us, paused and then started again. At times it was as if somebody was throwing buckets of water sideways at our tent. It continued to rain most of the night and still dark when I had to go out and pee. I waited for a lull, then cautiously opened the tent flap and stepped into a cold puddle. There was water everywhere. As soon as I finished it started to rain – a steady heavy downpour.

Day 3: I must have fallen asleep again because upon awakening it was soft grey outside. Stayed in the tent until 8:00 a.m. and finally looked out. Cold and cloudy. Roanne was very positive about walking to Summit Lake while I thought about walking out. Our car was at New Fork and it would have been easier to go ahead with our plans so when a bit of blue appeared in the otherwise overcast ceiling, the two of us dressed in all our clothes and while she made breakfast, I packed up and stretched the tent over some large, almost dry rocks on the hill above, weighting it down with rocks. It was windy and perhaps the nylon would dry enough – just the seams and floor needed time. Finally left at 9:45 a.m.

On the way up and out of Island Lake the realization that I had wrapped the wrong leg caused me to laugh out loud. Where was my mind for me to do that? My other knee was also quite sore but not half as bad as my right one. Almost embarrassed to tell Roanne except that a mother's mistakes are important to share so that our image of perfection is not so threatening. At the top of the ridge I re-strapped my leg and continued to wonder how such an error could have been made. Perhaps the inclement weather for one and the fact that the Highline Trail was above treeline most of the way with no shelter was enough for the degree of concern.

At the Elbow Lake signpost we turned north and, following the undulating trail down a draw, up and around some ponds, along streams running every which way, finally arrived at Fremont Crossing with its substantial bridge, one of the few in the Winds. Up ahead the country rose in what looked like an impassable wall. Lower Jean Lake which appeared two miles later after a climb of five-hundred feet, was as beautiful as I had remembered. When you think you're alone, it was a surprise to see a person in the distance perched on an outcrop that extended into the middle of the lake. 12,198-foot Stroud Peak rose in the north. A gradual climb around the lake eventually brought us to Upper Jean, not as impressive as its lower counterpart, where the trail continued above its west shore, then dropped to Lake 10,935 feet and climbed two hundred feet to the pass.

This had been a long, cold, windy walk and it was a great relief to see the wooden sign at the junction of the Shannon Pass Trail leading north towards Peak Lake. Surrounding us were 12,000- to 13,000-foot peaks – Mt. Oeneis and Sky Pilot Peaks to the north, Elbow Peak to the south, Bow Mountain, Mt. Arrow-head and Henderson to the east, a rocky landscape of soft grey and beige, charcoal and umber. Turning west into the rugged, boulder-strewn, exposed basin that held Elbow Lake, hungry and exhausted, a sheltered spot to have lunch was found.

In a tiny depression amongst the rocks and stunted bushes, bundled up in everything from our backpack, a hurried snack of bread and tahini (the tahini spread on with gloved fingers) offered warmth and allowed us to continue, more relaxed. After traveling along a high ledge that plunged to the lake far below, the two of us started the five-hundred-foot descent into a rocky draw, through spruce and whitebark pine, crossed Elbow Creek, and up and down for what seemed relentless miles of rolling country. At one point you could see the depression where Summit Lake was situated, still quite far-off.

Passed the cutoff to Sauerkraut and Bridger Lakes toward the south, dropped to a log bridge spanning Elbow Creek and up again through a thick forest where it was snowing lightly. The dark crevice of Pine Creek Canyon wound southwest toward Elkhart Park as Ro and I climbed, for the last time, to the rolling alpine meadows cradling Summit Lake. The flakes were larger and thicker up here and it was decided, before settling for a site, to make sure where the Palmer Lake Trail was located so that, in case of a heavy snowfall, our site would be next to the

trail that would take us out of the mountains. Walked around
the lake, saw another tent in the distance and chose a flat spot
close to some trees near the path.

Our tent was up just in time for the ground to stay dry under
it. Erecting a cooking shelter with Roanne's poncho within a nest
of trees was impossible because it was too cold to tie the edges
onto branches, our fingers and the cord would not bend easily,
and the snow was weighing down the middle of the poncho too
quickly. We gave that up and hurried down to a small lake
below to filter water. Of all times for the plunger not to work! It
was probably frozen. Ro and I manually collected water and
decided to boil it.

By this time it was snowing earnestly and the tent was
totally covered. I shook it and troweled the snow away from the
edges where it had slid to the ground. Sachi ran around outside,
delighted with all the white fluffy stuff. Roanne made some hot
tea and finally, relaxing in our down bags, warmed our freezing
hands and feet. Her boots were still wet from the day before and
she was glad to get them off along with the plastic bags she had
used to keep her socks dry. I was a bit concerned about the snow
but then I am always concerned about the weather. It was so
good to be in the tent that I almost didn't care about the walk out
tomorrow.

While peering over our maps, sipping tea and munching on
oat bars and roasted pumpkin seeds, a warm dinner was
cooking. If it was clear, the higher, shorter Doubletop Mountain
Trail would be the way to go; if not, the Palmer Canyon Trail
and New Fork Park in the trees would be our choice, that is, if
the path could be found at all. By now there was an outrageous
blizzard which could bury the tent and smother us and we
wouldn't have to worry about which way to walk out.

It was cold while hanging our food and emptying our
bladders. Sachi ran around in the blowing snow and did the
same. The light was fading, the snow was steady, and our
surroundings had shrunk to a few feet around the tent. The
meadows and peaks around Summit Lake had disappeared
leaving us in a white world – soft, peaceful, ethereal.

Settling in for a long night, Sachi curled up on her blanket, enveloped in our down vests, an attempt to stop her shivering. Roanne fell asleep for a few hours. The wind blew, the tent ballooned and the temperature dropped. I worried about getting out the next morning but remembered Finis Mitchell's words: "Early September storms pass quickly, you just have to sit them out."

Another thought surfaced about descending to Trapper Lake via the Pine Creek Canyon Trail, in the trees, instead of the Doubletop Mountain Trail. I hoped any trail could be found. We stayed warm, cinching our bags tightly around our heads. The hours passed slowly. I meditated, starting with my forgiveness prayer and sent loving kindness to everybody I knew and then to those I didn't. The night wore on. I could see, through our screening that ran around the bottom sides of the tent, that no more snow was accumulating. The ground was covered and the rocks glistened in the crystalline atmosphere.

Day 4: At 7:30 a.m. when I went out to answer the call of nature and get the food bag which was hanging in a fir tree about fifty feet from our site, the sky was blue. Icy snow on the ground, Summit Lake shrouded in mist, cold and clear, and it was going to be okay. Roanne made breakfast – hot Tahitian vanilla tea, cooked barley flakes, stevia and raisins. The tent was warm and our socks and gloves hanging from a cord strung inside the tent were almost dry. The sun appeared just before 8:00 a.m., finally surmounting the cloud cover. Luck was with us. But when I looked again a bit later clouds had moved in and I mentioned that it might be a good idea to leave as soon as possible.

Starting up the Doubletop Mountain Trail just after 9:00 a.m., a climb towards No Name Lakes, down and up to Cutthroat Lakes, down and up for another two miles, and finally, out of the snow, a descent to Palmer Lake where a stop was made for lunch. It was cold and windy and our maps came out to make the final decision as to what to do. The sky was overcast, some snow flurries and since the Doubletop Mountain Trail was above timberline (for the first four miles), it was decided to stay in the trees and descend Palmer Canyon to New Fork Park. Having come up this treacherous trail once before, it would be a lot easier going down.

After a quick lunch and a short climb to a small divide, Ro and I descended into the trees. It was steep and got steeper while switchbacking down the thickly forested north side of the canyon, its sheer granite walls reaching 1,500 feet skyward. Sachi ran ahead, waited for us to catch up and then took off again. It was at the bottom, just before the Reynold's Creek crossing, that a couple came toward us and, out of breath, told us that they had just encountered a very large grizzly a few yards back. Yes, they were sure it was a grizzly. They had startled it and it took off up the side of a hill and disappeared. I asked them exactly where this had happened. About three hundred yards up the trail . . . finally abolishing the common wisdom that there weren't any grizzlies in the Winds. I was nervous.

The two of us continued, cautiously, singing and talking loud in between short yelps for miles, not slowing down as the mile-and-a-half meadow of New Fork Park was crossed where the bear might be; howling, whistling and generally doing what we never do in the mountains: make noise. And then suddenly, in the middle of the trail, two large moose appeared that made us freeze in our tracks. The mama moved into the trees but the huge bull didn't budge, even with our shouting and hand clapping. Starting towards him, he abruptly moved up the hill, stopping behind a tree. A few steps forward and he retreated again. Finally working up the courage to pass them, Roanne and I consciously continued down the sheer, granite-walled canyon.

On and on we pushed, descending gradually over bedrock smoothed by ancient glaciers, through open slopes dotted with irregular boulders and a scattering of aspen, whitebark and lodgepole pine. Emerging from the trees, the lakes came into view in the distance. Tracing the trail through the folds of forested slopes on the north side of the canyon, my figuring gave us at least three to four miles to go, maybe more. Disconcerted, we walked on . . . and on . . . and on, descending gradually as the twisting canyon began to narrow.

A wooden sign appeared, always a welcome sight, and the boundary was crossed, leaving the wilderness behind. Our world was about to change.

After the Doubletop Mountain Trail cutoff, the sandy beach appeared. Dropping to our knees in sand, the little food left was devoured. Another mile around the upper lake, across sagebrush slopes usually covered with balsamroot at the beginning of summer, through aspen groves, brought us to the Narrows Campground and our car. A happy sight!

This trip, our last of the summer, was quite an adventure. Between the extremes of weather, the endless walking and the wildlife, Roanne and I said goodbye to the mountains, having done ourselves in.

Four days after arriving home, our world changed again. On September 11th, the Twin Towers of the World Trade Center in New York City were bombed by two planes; the Pentagon outside of Washington was next as well as an attempt on the White House which was evacuated. The Canadian and Mexican borders were closed. The United States responded to the attacks by launching a War on Terrorism and enacting the Patriot Act.

XX

North Fork Lake

August, 2002:

On August 8th Roanne arrived from New Mexico ready for a walk in the Winds. The ten-mile, washboard, dirt road took us to Boulder Lake and the canyon trailhead, the lowest in the Wind River Range – the first being Scab Creek. After hiding an extra key under the front bumper of her Volkswagon Bug and re-checking our packs, the two of us started the four-and-a-half-mile hike through the 1,100-foot granite walls of beautiful Boulder Canyon, at times alongside the creek which drained the bulk of the central Wind Rivers, but more often, high above the creek on sunny slopes scattered with limber pine and aspen; past the old beaver ponds at the head of the canyon where the cliffs narrowed, the 2000-foot, two-mile climb to Lake Ethel began. I thought I was going to die.

While looking for a sign at the top by the lake a couple from Prescott, Arizona said that it was about twenty feet back, lying in the bushes. Isn't that where it should be? Back in the wilderness again – this time heading for North Fork Lake, a large timberline body of water, one of the gems of the central Wind Rivers, and would be there the next day.

We left Lake Ethel, surrounded by blackened snags from the 1988 Fayette fire, and continued through lavender fireweed-carpeted slopes in the burned, barren forest to Ed's Lake, more like a shallow pond, and had lunch; proceeded up the draw to Lake Christina and a wonderful campsite among spruce and lodgepole pine with only one other tent about one hundred yards away. After filtering water Ro and I sat by the lake, totally exhausted. My hips and shoulders were sore as was her left foot.

While Lola, Roanne's new dog whom she had inherited in
Taos, ran around, the tent went up and dinner started. The
occupants of the other tent were returning and, as one of the
guys passed us, Lola chased him. She meant no harm of course,
just wanted to play, but he ran frantically, yelling that a dog was
after him. All in all, eight people eventually ended up at that site,
loud and intrusive, which continued on into the night.

Ro and I talked about her latest relationship – about
commitments, different points of view, male perceptions and her
feelings. Her boyfriend had left for the summer and wanted a
commitment but she wasn't prepared to commit. And why
should she feel guilty? Some guys want everything, take all they
can get and give little. Did he cause those feelings or were they
acquired from her female role model – me, not acquiescing to a
man's demands and feeling guilty about it. Do all women feel
that our God-given role is to please a man no matter how we
feel?

Both of us fell asleep with Lola in the tent but awoke when
she started to pace and, after she threw up, Roanne put her
outside. She connected all our straps to make a long leash and
tied her to a tree where she scratched around until she created a
shallow hollow and settled down. I fell into a relaxed sleep again
while the snoring continued from the other tent. Suddenly a
huge splash woke me, followed by something thrashing about in
the water, then silence again. It was 4:00 a.m. I looked out, saw
nothing and went back to sleep. Roanne hadn't heard anything.
Lola didn't even bark or growl.

Day 2: Light filtered through the darkness at 5:00 a.m. Dozed
on and off until 8:00 a.m. Calm and quiet. It's a special time,
those early morning hours, when the sounds of nature take
precedence. The stir of another day occurs gradually, picking up
momentum as the sun rises and brings yang energy to the scene.
In a tent you can hear this blossoming. I'd like to stay until the
flower blooms.

Just as the two of us started out on the trail two hikers
appeared. They had just seen a grizzly less than a half mile

back and it dawned on me that he was the big splash during the night. It was definitely time for my bear bell to come out.

The climb was steady through rocky dales to Perry's Lake and then up to larger Mac's Lake, buoyed in a basin of muted yellows and greens and I kept my ears tuned and eyes probing dense forest and cave-like crevices. My shoulders and hips ached and I wanted to stop but I knew that after a continuous ascent of four-and-a-half miles, we'd hit the Highline Trail and the alpine would be reached – open and high.

The peaks suddenly came into view and after two more miles along this well-traveled route, 9,754-feet North Fork Lake appeared. Walking around to the east side a site was found on a grassy ledge amongst plaited limber pines. The wind forced us to move the tent into the shelter of a broad stunted thicket facing east and the rising sun. Lola dug her hollow in the barbed branches just behind the tent, happy to get out of the wind. While settling in, a group of hikers approached and asked if we were camping there, saying it was the best spot in the valley. They said a cold front was moving in. I hoped it wouldn't snow and became apprehensive about the Hay Pass Trail – the lowest of the high passes over the Divide that we were planning to cross. I would like to wait for better weather.

Roanne started dinner and the wind continued.

Day 3: 6:00 a.m. A chorus of coyotes, voices, laughter and clanging pots. Sounds carry in the backcountry. Dozed until 7:30 a.m. when the sun was up, and after breakfast, filled a pack with lunch, maps, water filter, knife, journals, pens, dog bones, first-aid kit, and left for Hall's Lake.

Picking up the Fremont Trail east of our campsite, we hiked south to the cutoff for Europe Canyon, passing a large cairn, not sure where that obscure path led, and continued for another mile or so to an unmarked fork, realizing that the path at the cairn was probably the right one to take. The trail passed through a steep, rocky defile that I remembered from years back and, at another unmarked fork, turned right on what became a faint path which disappeared periodically; up a steep divide and at

10,816 feet walked down to a pretty lake thinking it was Hall's to get out of the wind for lunch. In the shelter of a large boulder Lola wet her toes and Roanne took a quick dip in the frigid water. While pouring over our topographic map, I realized that this lake wasn't big enough to be Hall's.

Traveling along the east flank of Medina Mountain, around the edge of the lake, we crossed its outlet and faced an extensive boulder field, and then another, even larger than the first. The wind was cold and unremitting, forcing us to don our hooded jackets. Stayed high on a broad ledge over the next few ridges until Hall's Lake came into view. To the south stretched the vast Boulder-Bonneville Basin, bordered by the Pronghorn Peaks and those of the East Fork Valley on the east. Pipe Organ, a peak southeast of Hall's Mountain on the Divide, was visible for the first time, as was the tip of Middle Fork Lake in the next valley. The wind tore my green Canadian Emerald Lake cap off my head and I searched the area below the high ridge I was sitting on. It took a few minutes to realize that it was gone for good – it had been with me for many years. But as Roanne would say, "Ke Garne" in Nepali, meaning "What to do! "

Clouds tumbled over the far mountains. The weather was definitely moving in as Ro and I climbed back to the Divide where the hikers who had wanted our campsite yesterday were struggling against the wind as well. One of the men, who introduced himself as Ken, hoped I didn't mind his asking how old I was and when I said sixty-one he thought it was great. He was fifty-two and figured he still had a few years to do what he was doing. They had talked about us the night before and had guessed that this was a mother/daughter team and that Roanne was about thirty-four. She was! He was the Wyoming State Public Defender and I recognized in him the passion I felt for these mountains. He had hiked to many of the areas familiar to us and when I mentioned my last book, "Within the Earth a Mountain," that recounted some of our hikes in the Winds, he took out a notepad in which I signed my name and address and told me he'd send me a check. He wanted an autographed copy.

Ro, me and Lola above Hall's Lake

Retracing our steps put us at our tent at 5:00 p.m., just in time to move it back under the trees before it started to rain and hail. Tea along with Roanne's oat bars was delightful while sitting on a rock in the aftermath of the storm watching the clouds dissolve. It was turning cold. After dinner in the tent, the front and back flaps were opened to let the smell out, then the food bags were moved because they were hanging too close to our new site, which left us laughing hysterically at missing the tree a few times and then getting the cord hung up in the branches.

Climbing into our bags at 9:00 p.m. and lighting a lantern, I listened to Roanne recite her poems she had to memorize for her upcoming performance in Manhattan, New York, a week after our trip. She talked about her life in Taos, her songwriter group, college courses and her desire to get a B.A., why I carved marble and what gave me the impetus to have changed my medium from painting to stone. Too physically tired to relax totally, our leg muscles tight and sore, both of us were overtaken by sleep at around 10:30 p.m. Lola slept at our feet and never moved. Quiet, no wind.

Day 4: It was cold at 5:00 a.m. and our breath crystallized in the soft grayness; mist on the glassy lake, sparse clouds to the north. While listening to coyotes in the distance and waiting for morning light, a decision to hang out rather than try for Hay's Pass sounded good.

Standing on a mat outside, Ro and I did some Do-In, one of the ancient traditional self-exercises to develop physical health, mental serenity and spiritual heights. Arms swinging to either side hitting shoulders and kidneys, arms swinging forward and back, up on our toes, then bending alternate knees. This loosens the upper back which, among other things, is the pancreas and intestine meridians.

The twelve positions of the Sun Salutation are always a good stretch. The King of Oundh, India, after understanding the benefit of this exercise, taught it to his queen and together they demonstrated it throughout their state, making it a compulsory part of physical training programs in the schools. Then we sat on our pads and, holding our big toes with knees bent and legs crossed, we rocked back and forth, leg stretches, back bends, sit-ups and hitting legs down along the outside – gall bladder meridian – and the inside – liver-spleen; then arms for all meridians – lung, large intestine, triple heater and heart governor.

After breakfast we packed a lunch, dressed in all our warm clothes, and left at 9:45 a.m. to find the Hay Pass Trail for an early start the next morning. Walking back along the Highline to where it splits to Hat Pass as the Fremont Trail, the marker was found, designating the Hay Pass Trail, an old sheep track which, until the sixties, was the only access to the valleys east of the Divide known only to a few solitary wanderers and sheep-herders who drove their flocks across the 10,960-foot pass.

Continuing up and out of the North Fork Valley, a great site was spotted for our last night just off the path leading out of the valley so that a walk around the lake on our way out the next morning was not necessary. High on a hill while sharing some apricots and almonds I photographed some horses and burros in a field with a blue tent in the trees.

Ro's socks drying

Back at the lake, a rocky inlet out of the wind captured us for a few hours. Lola found her spot in the grass and as she dozed the two of us enjoyed lunch. Soaking our feet and rubbing them on a rock to remove rough skin on our heels was therapeutic. Ro washed her socks and laid them on a rock to dry.

A loose, lacy cloud umbrella converged over Medina Mountain. The wind picked up and then stopped. The time passed slowly and I thought about Marty and whether the contractor had showed up to dig the foundation for the cabin he was going to move onto the lower two-and-a-half acres since our house on the ten acres above had sold. I sent a prayer to him for everything to run smoothly.

Roanne was memorizing her poetry while I sat staring across the lake to the Divide peaks. A cold front had moved in last night and, being midway through the trip with four more days to go, wondered for how long. I hoped the weather would hold for Hay Pass and worried about getting stuck on the other side.

Europe Peak

It was easy being with Roanne. She wanted this trip even more than I did. It's important to stop everything – do nothing. Thoughts never ceased. Yearning is never fulfilled. She gets up light and happy. I get up more serious, more burdened. I'm glad for her. I wonder if this is a state of being for me, if it has always been like this.

Back at the tent at 3:00 p.m. for bancha tea, a fruit bar and a back massage. Watched people come and go through her binoculars. After a delicious dinner of couscous, veggies, miso, mertensia leaves, lotus root slices and grated mochi, a stroll to the two other campsites which had been occupied for the last two nights but were now vacant, was refreshing. Ours was the best. Ro and I sat on a rock and watched the stretch of pink clouds fade and then, at around 9:00 p.m., got into our bags.

Roanne felt strange. We started to talk and ended up changing our plans. Not wanting to conquer the world, having a hard time softening our goals, a decision to just hike up Hay Pass rather than over – no heavy packs – was made. Her feet were in bad shape, and with a heavy load, she would be in constant pain. If the weather changed after crossing the Divide there wasn't enough time to wait it out. Too much climbing with no days of rest. The relaxing day just spent was wonderful. The Brown Cliffs would have to wait for a special trip just to see them specifically. They were too remote. Changing plans was our way of life.

Day 5: 6:35 a.m. It was calm, the lake still, and the sky clear. As soon as the sun rose, the wind picked up. The coyotes were close this morning and I was glad Lola was in the tent. They seemed to be in the meadow north of us just below the ledge our tent was on. I am more relaxed during the night with Lola along. She would likely hear something long before I would.

Over breakfast we talked again about our decision. Was I happy with it? I had mixed emotions. I knew it was a healthy choice but I had to override my "summit fever" as Roanne called it – the striving to do more, go on, go farther – instead of relaxing and enjoying the moment. Slowing down is what it's all about. I wanted to see the Fortress, the Brown Cliffs, the lakes on the other side. I'm torn between my yearnings and the wisdom that's so difficult to accept. Roanne has more of a pull not to pack up but the lure of the high country is there. So we'll get up into the heights to satisfy that drive and come back down to our site, replenished, fulfilling that intense need to "go for it" always. "More is not always better," as Marty says, "it's just more."

The way to do this hike up Boulder Canyon to North Fork Lake is to have a drop pack at the lake saving one of the two days and energy it takes to walk in. The two of us talked about the Brown Cliffs on every trip and never quite got there. They remained out of our reach – an enigma – like my birth mother.

9:30 a.m. Roanne prodded me to get up and go while reclining in the tent and stretching her left leg above her head. I needed to rest after a huge breakfast. Lola had a distemper shot just before the trip and Roanne had to get some homeopathic pills into her so that she didn't have too much of a reaction while in the wilderness. I have never had such love for an animal and I marvel at her.

Packed up and left at 10:00 a.m. for the Hay Pass Trail, hiked around Lake Victor and up the North Fork to a broad, flat, rocky, barren pass. Angel Peak to the west (we were on the other side of Angel Peak in Bald Mountain Basin exactly two years ago wanting to see the Brown Cliffs), Dennis Lake, below and at the very bottom, one of the Golden Lakes – glad to have made the decision to day hike. The wind sent us back over the pass for lunch to a lake where a sheltered spot between some boulders appeared.

"Could we take a picture of us both sitting here?" I asked Roanne.

"If you want to take it, do it!" Roanne replied. "Don't ask. Instead of asking if we can, can't you just say, let's take a picture. Wanna do this? No, I don't want to. But if you want me to, I'll do it."

Wow! What was this all about? OK. A deep-seated issue had surfaced. This might be a good time to deal with it.

What I need to say is "I want to take a picture" and not put the responsibility on her for my decision so I don't impose on her. I don't like to ask anybody to do anything for me. It must come from my childhood, being afraid to ask for help. The bad feelings persisted over lunch. She said not to hang onto it. She just had to tell me because this is what gets her crazy. It left me thinking about my shortcomings all the way down the trail, not really understanding the essence of my hang-up. I'm afraid to ask for fear of being turned down so I shift the responsibility onto another and let them have to say no, and, of course, they feel obligated to do what I want because they, in turn, are afraid to say no. So I have to say what I want and take the risk of being turned down.

I drank the last drops of our water high in the canyon, then filled up with water to filter back at the tent. While walking, strange clouds had formed ahead, seemingly over the valley where our tent was situated. The rest of the sky was clear.

Smoke! It couldn't be anything other than smoke – rusty grey –
coming from the direction of North Fork Lake. Would we have
to pack up after an exhaustive fourteen-mile hike and start
down?

The smoggy cloud behind the southern ridge of the valley
was still too close for comfort. There didn't seem to be anybody
left in the area and I wondered if a ranger had been around to
evacuate. Dinner in the tent to get out of the wind.

I was ready to leave the next day, anxious to get out. I'd had
enough of the wind. Roanne was okay with that but wanted to
wait until morning to decide. I adjusted her upper back (chiro-
practically) and she ran through her poems. Suddenly a noise
startled us. The back rain flap had been raised. A deer passed
and then came round to the front. She stared at us and finally
wandered off to the creek below. Lola slept through the whole
thing. She certainly couldn't warn us of anything in her state. I
think the hike took it out of her.

Roanne fell asleep quickly while I tossed and turned,
listening. I must have fallen asleep because when I looked at my
watch, it was after 3:00 a.m. Lola growled just before light.

Mt. Victor

Day 6: A clear blue sky made our decision to stay easy and we opted for the sandy beach at Victor Lake. Everything was packed and moved to the knoll on the other side of the valley to get an early start in the morning. As the tent was being erected two fat cowboys on horses, camped in the high meadow where the blue tent had been the other day, wanted to know if they could take their horses up Europe Canyon. I told them it was narrow and steep but I thought they could make it. They had called about the fire at Divide Lake off the Scab Creek Trail and had to change their plans and come in on the Boulder Lake Trailhead. Scab Creek was a canyon to the south and still at a safe distance from us.

Ro and Lola

A relaxing, playful day at the lake. Back at our new site the two of us sat on a mat, leaned against a broad boulder and watched the opposite hills drop into shadow. Suddenly the peaks turned red and glowed – just long enough to take a few pictures. I wondered as I stared into the distance if Long Lake was in front of Europe Peak or behind. I'd wait to get back in the tent to look at the map again.

Day 7: Up at 6:00 a.m. to a clear, blue sky, some elongated cloud to the south over the fire area. I was comfortable during the night but slept in spurts. Up at 3:30 a.m. and 5:00 a.m., always surprised when my watch indicated that one-and-a-half to two hours had passed. Lola growled and then all was quiet. Waited for the sun, as always. It'll take the day to walk out to which I am looking forward – to the walking, not the leaving.

The sun appeared at 7:07 a.m. over the south end of Horseshoe Ridge and the tent glowed. Roanne transferred our trash into a smaller bag – 16 oz. If everybody had this much garbage per week the planet would breathe easier.

Packed up after breakfast and started the eleven-mile hike out. Our packs were heavy and the thought of growing older and not being able to carry such a load anymore bothered me. Suddenly I fell flat on my face – scraped my knee and hurt my wrist. Another fall. It was after still another that the realization of my new rather stiff, bulky boots might be the cause. Since purchasing them I have been falling frequently.

Upon our return home I mailed my book to Ken and a few weeks later received a very sensitive response. He wrote in great detail about the book.

Dear Harriet (and Ro):

I just finished reading "Within the Earth a Mountain." A most delightful read! It can't be easy to be willing to share your thoughts with strangers. While portions of the book are on my mind, I thought I would share them with you.

When I go backpacking, I always like to pick a campsite such that I have a "room with a view." When we ran into you two at North Fork Lake, I was envious that you had a choice campsite. But, after reading your book, I was glad that we really wanted a location not next door to our neighbors.

(Quoted from my book):
"Then a strange thing happened. A couple walked up to us and asked if they could share our campsite. We looked at each other not quite sure they had asked what they did. I told them there were lots of campsites farther on. They looked surprised that we didn't want company and left. I call that the herding instinct. We resumed our dinner feeling intruded upon. There is so little privacy in the world. Isn't that why people go into the mountains?"

My sentiments exactly! You both were forgiven for taking the "room with a view" as we chatted with you at the pass into Hall's Lake Basin. When I read about Ro losing her favorite John Deere cap on her first trip into the Tetons, I was again sorry that we never found Harriet's at Hall's Lake.

I had to chuckle when I read about your experience at getting kicked out of your campsite overlooking Island Lake. I have camped there at least three, maybe four times, in the last twenty years – always at the same campsite. The view across the lake to Fremont Peak at sunset is spectacular! The last time I camped there (3 years or so ago), a summertime, college boy "wonder" ranger showed up and told us to move our tent. What a bunch of crap! You could not even see the tent on the knoll from the trail. Nevertheless, we moved. And, my opinion of the summer help hired by the U.S. Forest Service dropped even further! It's called power, position, and thinking that you know it all.

I really enjoyed your description of why people go into the mountains. You are able to express in words my exact feelings.

(Quoted from my book):
"Walking in the mountains is a unique experience. One becomes an integral part of nature. You see and hear things that you couldn't notice traveling by bike or car or, least of all, by plane. Our bodies are made to walk. It improves our circulation, increases our lung capacity, massages our meridians stimulating our nervous system, and promotes a general feeling of well-being. It doesn't cost anything. It gives us time

to think and to dream – both left and right brain experiences. Walking is wonderful and in a world of turmoil it offers peace and quiet.

"At the end of the day, after a long hike, my body tingling and mind quieted, I feel as if I've been away. I become sensitive to the ebb and flow of life, the crystalline images created by clear air, and conscious of a three-dimensional feeling of space around me. Any troubles, problems or doubts either seem more remote or have been resolved."

I also enjoyed the quotes and references to Finis Mitchell. In my treks into the Winds over the past 20 years or so, I have run into Finis twice at Elkhart Park, and I have a signed copy of his trail guide to the Winds. A most remarkable mountain man – may he rest in peace!

Please, please, please keep me on your mailing list for when you publish your book on your treks into the Winds. I definitely will want a signed copy!

Until our paths again cross . . .

Kindest Regards,
Ken Koski

P.S. Harriet, great artwork on the wild flowers! Thanks for the postcard. No doubt in my mind after reading your book that you know your wild flowers much better than I.

"If you are free, I recommend a hiking trip on a wilderness footpath. How inspiring it is to walk all day in the sunshine and sleep all night under the stars. What a wonderful experience in simple, natural living. Since you carry your food, sleeping equipment, etc., on your back, you learn quickly that unnecessary possessions are unnecessary burdens. You soon realize what the essentials of life are – such as warmth when you are cold, a dry spot on a rainy day, the simplest food when you are hungry, pure cool water when you are thirsty. You soon put material things in their proper place, realizing that they are there for use, but relinquishing them when they are not useful. You soon experience and learn to appreciate the great freedom of simplicity."

Peace Pilgrim

XXI

Desolation Valley

July 2003:

On July 29th at 10:10 a.m. Big Sandy Opening was crowded with cars, trucks and campers from all over the United States. There were sparse clouds when Roanne and I started out through the lodgepole pine forest along the banks of the Big Sandy River, heading for the Fremont Trail that would take us 5.1 miles to Dad's Lake and our first campsite. I had been working on our small cabin in Daniel, Wyoming at the bottom of the hill since the end of May and hadn't done any serious hiking. Roanne, too, had taken only a few five-mile walks around the outskirts of Taos where she was living. Not being in good shape we were going to take it slow and make it a short day.

After a half-mile the two of us turned north towards Meek's Lake, skirted its east shore and climbed gradually to cross the Bridger Wilderness boundary. Nice!

Flat-feathered fir, packaged pine and sharp-squared spruce – Roanne recited her identifying means to the evergreen trees that she had learned at Teton Science School in the Jackson Hole Valley.

Laturio Mountain to the east would soon be at our backs as our climb amongst cinquefoil, bistort, daisy, lupine and yarrow brought us to a broad, grassy area where suddenly the peaks of the East Fork Valley came into view bringing remembrances of past hikes. This valley to which I yearned to return since I had looked down into it from Pyramid Lake over a decade ago, was our goal. But our plans had not been formally discussed. She and I were just heading in that direction.

The trail passed through the forest-rimmed extensive meadow of Fish Creek Park, by Divide and Mirror Lakes, and finally descended a grassy draw to Dad's Lake – a large, irregular-shaped, island-dotted body of water. A flat site surrounded by trees on the west side of the lake appeared and camp was set up. Exhausted, both of us dozed in the tent after which Roanne swam in the frigid lake. Six guys moved in above us at an acceptable distance, and were sensitive enough to ask if they were too close. They hadn't seen us tucked away in the trees.

The leftover nori rolls made for lunch were finished while ramen cooked for dinner. Finding a tree to hang our food was easy. As the sun dropped, leaving the valley in shadow, some noisy girls moved in behind us and climbing the knoll to let them know we were there didn't make a difference.

Roanne adjusted my atlas-axis (first two vertebrae) and my headache faded. The maps came out, our favorite pastime, while birds chirped and thunder rolled around the Cirque of the Towers. A few light raindrops as dark clouds moved east over the Divide. After some stretches inside the tent Ro and I relaxed and listened to the wind.

I thought about Marty and wondered about the availability of that piece of land on the New Fork Lakes road next to the National Forest boundary. The tiny town of Daniel was getting built up. A subdivision next to our property was in the making and the lot next to us had become industrial with a lot of big trucks and earthmovers moving in – an indicator of things to come. I was glad to be in the Winds again.

Day 2: 7:00 a.m. Roanne was doing yoga on a rock by the lake – a true child of the wild, exuberant in the wilderness, and totally self-motivated. I attributed it to the alternative high school she had attended in Mendocino, California. I am lazier by nature, reluctant to get out of my bag, wanting only to read "Himalayan Odyssey," a tortuous trek across the spine of the highest mountains in the world. My neck is still out, the remains of a headache, and perhaps Ro will try adjusting it again today.

The sky was clear, the sun was up, the sounds were comforting. I slept quite well – up every two hours – but fell back to sleep easily. Lola being in the tent, like Sachi, makes me feel safe.

A mother duck submerged and her eight babies followed. She appeared and they surfaced, scattered, and immediately clustered around her, instinctively needing their mother. They waddled onto a rock, sunned themselves and re-entered the water, she at the helm. Three followed, then three more and finally two at the end.

Two guys fished on the far side of the lake while another in the tall grass watched. Tea and granola for me, just tea for Ro. I can eat only a bit. My body was absorbing the surroundings and digestion/hunger took second place. Dad's Lake was lovely. Lola ran around, in and out of the water, and stood guard while we rested on the rock.

9:30 a.m. Packed up and moved to higher realms. Lola's leash was lost. Some teenage boys and their leader let us pass and thought Lola sporting her packs was cool. Up a long, rocky, steep draw to the grasslands above the Washakie drainage and a breathtaking view of the 12,000-foot East Fork peaks – Geikie, Ambush, Raid, Bonneville, Tower, Hooker and Pyramid. Turned east for the two-and-a-half miles to our next campsite and hiked along broad, meandering Washakie Creek through meadows, scattered Engelmann spruce and whitebark pine. Lavender, yellow and white as far as the eye could see. Wolf's Head, Overhanging Tower, Shark's Nose and Block Tower in the Cirque disappeared as the two of us and Lola continued up the narrowing canyon to Shadow Lake, nestled in a timberline bowl at the foot of a massive granite wall, the backside of the Cirque. Roanne went in for a swim.

It took over two hours to settle on a site above the northwest shore, a bit confining, heavily treed, nothing level – and buggy! Hanging our food was formidable. There wasn't much of a choice of limbs but finally got it after about a dozen attempts. This was an excellent spot for lunch, not an overnight. We didn't know it at the time.

During the night I became claustrophobic and started to unzip the tent but because of the bugs converging on the screen, stopped cold and tried to talk myself out of it. Clutching at air and breathing deeply didn't get rid of the sensation. It's almost indescribable and quite puzzling when you can't calm yourself. Always apprehensive when preparing to climb a Divide pass could have forced this frantic feeling. Roanne, too, was up most of the night. Lola didn't even dig herself a hollow. She was uneasy, pacing in the tent. The area was too treed and we didn't feel good, probably the reason for the interminable time finding a spot.

Day 3: After making too much hot cereal, the remainder was placed in a seal-proof bag and hung with the rest of our food; packed lunch, water, map, dog bones, first aid kit and secured the tent. Following the trail around the lake we climbed to Billy's Lake – above treeline, beautiful and vast. Indian paintbrush, bluebells, Parry's primrose, lupine, wildflowers not seen at lower elevations suddenly appeared in profusion – a lush landscape – and I wondered how we could exist without it.

Around Barren Lake to Texas Lake, the climb continued. Roanne who was up ahead suddenly shouted, "I'm not going to do that," her comment when she first glimpsed 11,640-foot Texas Pass. Staying high above the lake, we traversed a boulder field, converged onto a sandy, slippery path halfway up, and finally steep talus to the top. Forty minutes later found us – happy and relieved – on a broad, grassy divide overlooking Pingora, the rock in the middle of the Cirque of the Towers. One could see clear down the Popo Agie Valley, Lizard Head Peak and Big Sandy Pass (sometimes called Jackass Pass), the south entrance to the Cirque – beauty as far as the eye could see. Dropping down a bit on the south side, a small snowfield was crossed in order to look into the Cirque but Lonesome Lake, tucked beneath the steep cliff under our feet, could not be seen.

Climbing back across layers of rock to the top, the three of us started down the almost vertical path, and about half an hour later, reached the sandy beach at Texas Lake. Lunch was welcome while watching two couples pick their way around the lake towards the pass, one up the trail and the other horizontally across the boulder field like us. The first couple made it to the top in half the time. It's easier on a path.

Waterfall at Billy's Lake

The trail down to our site was not the one we came up, and a decision was made to move our tent to a more open area with a view of the lake. No bugs. After filtering water, Roanne cooked dinner while the two of us talked about where to go tomorrow: Skull Lake, Washakie Pass, East Fork Valley – a decision would be made in the morning.

Day 4: Another restless night. The people at the lake were extremely noisy. At around 5:00 a.m. Lola growled and woke us from a deep sleep. I peeked out and saw nothing. Up again at 7:00 a.m. for some yoga outside the tent. In one of my back-packing books it said that the Fremont Trail north from Big Sandy offered travelers the chance to escape the throngs of backpackers en route to the Cirque of the Towers and that Shadow Lake on the backside was a lot less busy. Not so.

Barley flakes, flaxseed and raisins for breakfast. There were a few white suggestions of clouds in clear blue. While packing,

Ro and I sat in the tent for a few minutes of blissful non-weight-bearing living.

11:00 a.m. Started out for Skull Lake, leaving a party of about twenty at the lake. When Lola realized that Washakie Creek was just down the valley, there was no holding her back. Off she went, ignoring our calls, and into the water, packs and all. Roanne caught her just in time and, proceeding north climbed three hundred feet in a bit less than a mile through a forest of Engelmann spruce, whitebark pine and subalpine fir to Skull Lake. Because the lake was swampy, our plan for Washakie Pass was abandoned and we continued up to Pyramid Lake.

"How many? How many are you keeping?" a guy shouted to his friend across the lake who had just caught a fish. People are seldom heard yelling like that in the wilderness. He was oblivious to our presence. Ro and I exchanged remarks in whispered tones. "I think it has a lot to do with the food people eat," she said; "it makes them loud, restless and chaotic. And that's only half the story. The rest is the way they're brought up, fighting for everything, unaware of their surroundings."

Up another draw to a grassy saddle just above Mae's Lake and the junction of the Hailey Pass Trail, a hike that Roanne, Karen and I had taken many years ago on our way back from the lakes east of the Divide. A steep climb through a narrow ravine brought us to Pyramid Lake above timberline. Beyond the one tent nestled on the side of a hill the trail came to an end. Another tent site in the tundra above the lake was not easy to find in this tiny, remote, high, barren valley. Lots of bugs.

Dinner was cooked outside while the breeze blew the bugs away, eaten inside, then our food was hung off a large boulder – no tall trees. The East Fork peaks, Geikie, Ambush and Raid, were outrageous and when the sun dropped, we strolled to the edge of the bench overlooking the upper basin of the East Fork River and decided on tomorrow's trip. There were three tents at the edge, people milling about and a large bag of food on the top of a boulder.

Day 5: Our first peaceful night. Roanne started breakfast just before the sun rose at 7:30 a.m. and then made our lunch while the tea water boiled. I pulled my wool hat out of my pack for the first time. A hummingbird whizzed by while the two of us enjoyed hot cereal in the tent warmed by the sun.

Following the route that brought us to the edge yesterday, a descent into the East Fork River Basin which housed three beautiful lakes where a flat spot just above the river was found and camp set up amidst stunted spruce. A huge boulder quite a ways from our tent with a concave face was perfect for hanging our food. Wildflowers as far as the eye could see. We packed lunch, pants, jacket, water and hiked to the upper lake at the foot of Mt. Bonneville, hopped boulders to the back of the lake and ate on a large slab that gently disappeared into the water. Because the water smelled fishy, we hiked down to the middle lake for a swim. Heavy clouds had moved in and I wanted to get closer to our tent. On our return, the five hikers camped yesterday on the bench were making their way out of the valley.

Some apricots and almonds were devoured while sitting on a rock by the outlet stream. Roanne swam, Lola slept and I waded in the shallows; then sat on a rock and for two heavenly hours, did nothing; covered up from the sun; talking about how important it was for us to hike into the high country to the trail's end and be alone at least once a summer; and about walking all the way out tomorrow because Dad's Lake might be too busy on the weekend.

Day 6: Peaceful night. Cloudy. We had the valley to ourselves. I was up a lot during the night, then dozed until 6:00 a.m. when Roanne got up.

She asked what worried me. I thought and couldn't decide. Karen's life, a repetition of mine with a divorce, two daughters and an irrational husband; ultimately, the warming of the planet, the disappearing water resources, and the ineptness and unconcern of the government.

The walk out was long and enjoyable; a whole different perspective from that of hiking in; a few drops of rain, enough for us to cover our packs and don our waterproof jackets. The trail was difficult to find but finally a depression of a path appeared. A NOLS group approached while Ro and I were picking mertensia leaves. The leader told us that they had been in Desolation Valley. I hadn't heard of it. He said it was another name for the East Fork River Valley. I vaguely remembered somebody referring to it by that name. Desolation Valley. Desolate, for sure. Where can you go in the Winds and have a whole valley to yourself in the middle of summer?

Desolation Canyon, Pyramid Peak in background

This trip was easy. No heavy family talk. No tension between us. Just did what we liked, together.
That was to be our last backpacking trip although she and I still day-hiked together all the time.

Our Daniel house on the two-and-a-half acres sold, we purchased the ten acres on the New Fork Road next to the National Forest to keep a foot in the Winds, and Marty and I relocated to Taos, New Mexico, where Roanne and her boyfriend had moved in together.

The Wilderness in Our Genes

"Going to the wilderness is going home. The mapping of the human genome confirmed that, genetically, we are still wild, Pleistocene creatures. Finally – an answer to why we feel so at home in the wilderness.

"We are a genetic library of gifts informed by centuries of life in the wilderness; gifts from the experiences of antecedent creatures ichthyian, reptilian, and mammalian, which still lie in our brainstem; gifts from the struggles of the naked ape with neither fang nor claw who was able, not only to survive, but to flourish – simply and elegantly – in wild landscapes.

"When we first walk into wilderness, we feel like alien creatures, but if we stay a while, usually about a week, those gifts become apparent.

"We become aware that our eyes see better: we can pick things out in the landscape more keenly; we can measure distance more accurately; and shape, color and contrast are vividly apparent.

"Our noses discriminate and identify the odors on the wind: the smell of a bighorn is very different from that of a bear; and there is a marsh upwind.

"The sounds we heard on our first day came from a general direction but now our binaural senses are so keen we can almost pinpoint the source and distance of a sound – and identify it.

"The awkwardness we first felt when moving over broken ground has been replaced by a fluid, economical rhythm of movement that seems almost effortless.

"These are not new skills learned; they are ancient abilities recalled.

"We sense our relationships with the other creatures with whom we share these landscapes.

"As we peer into campfire flames, the comfort of thousands of fires in thousands of caves over thousands of years warms us from inside as from the outside.

"The warmth of the sun and the snap of the cold affirm that we are alive and vulnerable.

The mountains, the deserts, the storms, and the rivers challenge our cunning and demand our respect.

"As we lie on the Earth in the evening, the march of Orion across the heavens fixes us in time.

"We are still those Pleistocene creatures – at home and full of the wonder of being.

"This is the wildness in our genes, found manifest in a peace that transcends time and in a place we shall always need
– wilderness."

George Duffy

XXII

Lady and the Llamas

July 2002: A year earlier . . .
Since Marty couldn't carry a pack and Roanne was living in New
Mexico, I had no way of getting into the mountains. Marty and I
did some day hikes until we discovered that the Outdoor Shop
in Pinedale rented llamas to hikers wanting an easy, weightless
way into the Winds.

It had taken one hour for Rex, owner of the shop, to prepare
his truck for us to drive to the trailhead as well as answer all our
questions, having never worked with llamas before – important
points on traveling, feeding, staking so they would stay close,
and generally living with them in the mountains. The panniers
he had given us to take home the day before were packed with
our food and clothing, and balanced – weighing the same on
both sides – as he had instructed us; ready to roll at 11:15 a.m. for
a three-day hike into the Winds with his llamas, Coco and Willie,
and Lady, our newly-acquired border collie.

"I knew I forgot something on the way in," was the first
comment from a hiker who was on her way out, referring to the
llamas; "that's what I need," was another; "traveling in style,"
and "I'm going to trade him in," was the last comment from a
lady hiking with a guy when she saw the llamas. They were
well-behaved, didn't spook when other hikers passed and were
used to giving horses the right of way.

Larkspur, lupine, Indian paintbrush and millions of buttercups along the trail; iridescent fleabane, heartleaf arnica,
bluebells by a stream; and Big Sandy Lake at 3:15 p.m. I was
happy to be back in the wilderness again.

One more mile to Clear Lake through a timberline forest of
whitebark pine and spruce and our campsite from the year

before. We unloaded the llamas, got them settled with grass, water and food, set up the tent, filtered water and found a tree to hang our food. Leftovers from lunch were devoured while sitting on a rock terrace staring into the west, watching a storm move in.

Settling into our tent at 6:00 p.m. and munching on some dried strawberries, I thought about Roanne on a backpack trip in the Grand Tetons when she was very young. I found her sitting on a rock, staring into space, eating dried strawberries out of the bag – her fingers, mouth, cheeks and tip of her nose stained red. She loved strawberries, dried or fresh – and I felt lonely for her.

The two of us relaxed, I leaning on Lady, while the alpenglow on Haystack, Temple and East Temple faded quickly to dusty pewter. It was difficult getting to sleep because of the lightning and thunder. A light drizzle between 2:00 a.m. and 4:00 a.m. was comforting although the lightning and rumbling continued throughout the night; up at 6:00 a.m. and dozed luxuriously until 8:00 a.m.

Day 2: After breakfast and packing a lunch all of us left for the open, alpine basin that housed Deep Lake, a mile up the valley. East Temple Peak, the Spike and Temple Peak, the second highest of the southern Wind Rivers, loomed ahead.

The llamas were staked, Marty and I had lunch while Lady played in the water, then hiked to the saddle overlooking Temple Lake. Some homemade bars were devoured while sitting on a rock high above the lake. Marty photographed a display of shooting stars and I sketched the monkeyflowers at the waterfall. Descending this narrow valley, the Cirque and Pingora could be seen in the distance.

After a tasty meal and the dishes washed the two of us wandered amongst the trees and discovered an obscure path leading to the foot of mile-long Haystack Mountain. Lady slipped on a wet rock, limped a bit but recovered quickly.

Lots of mosquitoes. Luckily the wind blew them away. A crimson blush lit the surrounding peaks and Clear Lake turned silver.

Coco, Willie and me

Marty, Coco and Willie at Deep Lake, the Spike and East Temple Peak

The alpenglow faded and by 9:00 p.m. we were back in our tent reading, lulled to sleep by the sound of water rushing on rocks – a clear quiet night with only a few rumblings from afar.

Haystack Mountain; Marty, Coco, Willie and Lady leaving Clear Lake

Day 3: The next morning after a leisurely breakfast the panniers were packed and balanced, loaded on the llamas and all of us slowly walked out of this tiny valley. Willie and Coco were a big hit! People wanted to take their pictures and asked a lot of questions. It was no trouble getting them into the truck and Marty drove the long, bumpy, rutted, gravel road back to town.

We did it! It was fun! Would love to do it again, convinced this was the way to go, rather expensive, but the lodging was cheap.

XXIII

Living with Llamas

2002-2003:

Our friend Lou dropped by one day and told us that he had just delivered propane to a man south of Pinedale who asked him if he knew anybody wanting some llamas. He had over sixty of them at his ranch in Texas and had to get rid of a few. Lou immediately thought of us. After our trip into the Winds last year with Coco and Willie, Marty and I had talked about getting two of our own.

On August 1st, 2002, Ted from Texas stopped by. He spent his summers in Pinedale and, if we were really serious about his llamas, he would truck them from his ranch to Wyoming next summer. It was thirty years since I had handled large animals – I had owned a horse and boarded two others when I lived in Stowe, Vermont. Not especially being an animal person, I guess the need to get into the mountains was paramount for me. Marty loved animals – cats and dogs. This would be an adventure. Little did we know.

Ted said he would help with the training. Marty and I prepared for their arrival by building a corral off the shed with a sheltered stall to get them out of the hot Wyoming sun, loaded up with hay and llama food, and purchased a large rubber water container. Lou, in the meantime, found an old propane-run truck for transporting them.

At the end of June, two, one-year-old llamas arrived at our home in a huge downpour and were very reticent to leave the trailer. Ted finally got them to move out, after much prodding, and they tumbled into our corral which he felt wasn't adequate. They needed some time to get used to their new home and Ted said he would come back in about a week to help us reinforce the structure and show us how to halter them. Meanwhile we would get used to them being here.

They were as cute as can be, full of piss and vinegar. They became Daniel and Carson since we were traveling between Daniel, Wyoming and Carson, New Mexico (Carson was just outside of Taos). Carson was a bit larger and more delicate while Daniel, shorter and stockier.

Ted suggested that the two of us sit on chairs outside the corral and then, gradually move inside. They looked at us and wouldn't come close. Five days later they were eating out of our hands. That's not really saying much. It's like offering candy to a child.

Our first lesson – haltering them. They pushed Ted around quite a lot until he got tough enough and they gave in. I don't think we could have done this. It took another seven days for us to scratch Daniel's neck, two more days to take off Carson's halter, and the next day, scratch Carson's neck. They smelled like freshly mowed hay and were warm and cuddly.

Were we in over our heads with these guys? Even though they were small they were strong. I was a little reluctant about it, Marty a bit bolder. I wanted so badly for this to work.

Two weeks later Ted gave us our second lesson. It wasn't going to be easy to train them. I guess Marty felt like he was doing most of the work and finally complained that it wasn't his total responsibility. Not being as comfortable around them as he was, I thought I was helping out. The two of us had a long talk. I was brought up as a spoiled single child. But I'm a grownup now and have to learn to drop childish things. I did.

Towards the end of July, Ted came by to give us another lesson. By the end of the month Carson ventured out of the corral for a few moments; things were moving along.

A week later the two of them were on lead ropes walking around the field surrounding our cabin. Two and a half weeks after that Daniel jumped into the truck three times and Carson got halfway in twice. The next day Carson got into the truck and packing started for our return to New Mexico. At the end of the month both llamas got into the truck at the same time. Whew!

At the beginning of September Marty and I drove about ten feet with the llamas in the truck; then up the hill beside our house; then decided to buy a secondhand, two-horse trailer because we couldn't imagine traveling the thruways with these two animals hanging out the back of the truck. Even though it was enclosed with metal slats, the llamas seemed to tower over the top. Now their training began again to get them into the trailer, so different from the truck.

Two weeks later found us leaving our home in the early hours of the morning on our way to New Mexico. It wasn't easy to find a place to fill our truck with propane as well as finding a motel that would take llamas. The boys remained in the trailer overnight while we relaxed in a second-rate room.

Heading east through Colorado on Interstate 70 with heavy traffic on all sides while listening for any unusual sounds coming from the back was sheer madness. To say the two of us were totally anxiety-ridden is putting it mildly, and it was a huge relief to get off the thruway at Minturn where a turn south toward the steep, long, edgy climb to Leadville (over 10,000 feet) was negotiated, hoping to make it pulling such a heavy load. Finally crossed into New Mexico at Antonito, turned east at Tres Piedras, and arrived at our home in the early evening. The next day the corral and fencing at the back of our house were re-enforced while the llamas waited in the trailer.

On October 15th we walked two miles to the post office with Carson and Daniel and managed to hang on to them every time a car passed. Their training continued every day. On November 23rd they went crazy when the panniers that Ted had given to us were placed on their backs. After two more days they started to relax; and another few days until the straps could be attached to the underside of their bellies. That was an accomplishment! The next thing to do was to slowly load weight, a little every day, starting with one piece of firewood in each pannier. They didn't seem to mind.

In January 2004, the covered stall at the rear of our house was screened to protect the llamas from a wolf hanging out back. Six days later we walked the llamas with full packs (58 pounds each) along the Rio Grande Gorge Trail.

Marty picked up Daniel's front legs. I couldn't get myself to do that but I held on to him for dear life while he did it. Learning to cut their toenails was going to be next to impossible. We never got around to doing that. The vet did.

Everything was going well until the thing that the two of us were most apprehensive about happened. Marty and I arrived home from town to find the corral empty. After a few frantic hours a sudden movement in the far meadow, quite a ways from our house, caught our eyes. The two of us chased them for four hours and finally gave up because it was getting dark. The next morning, Marty and I, loaded for bear, or I should say llamas, with a pail of pellets and their lead ropes, walked to the spot where they were seen last. No llamas. After searching for what seemed forever, two ears suddenly appeared above the sagebrush.

Our approach was slow and steady. They got up and stared at us, totally unconcerned. We circled them, Marty on one side and me on the other, still a ways off. He shook the bucket of grain, enticing them, and Daniel took a step forward. The two of us crept closer. They didn't move. Marty kneeled down in the bushes and shook the pail again. Daniel took another step. It went on and on until Daniel was no more than a few yards away. Then Carson started to move and, little by little, caught up to Daniel. Marty threw the lead rope around Daniel's neck. Carson moved in cautiously. When he was close enough, I did the same. We returned home, relieved, and reinforced the corral again.

The next thing to do was get them used to being staked. A long spike was hammered into the ground and their lead ropes attached to it, one for each. They got tangled and had to be moved farther apart. Doing this once a day, it didn't take long for them to get the idea.

After buying a Nisson truck because it was too difficult finding fuel for the propane vehicle, Marty and I, Lady, Carson and Daniel left New Mexico at 5:00 a.m. and arrived in Wyoming at 9:00 p.m. The llamas took the drive well. We were exhausted.

The next day at our New Fork land, the llamas went back into training, this time streams being the issue. They definitely did not like getting their feet wet. But Daniel paved the way by eventually walking through the water while Carson jumped to the other side dragging me with him.

A few days later a trip to Middle Piney Lake, just west of Pinedale in the southern Wyoming Mountain Range, allowed us to walk through snow and rocks while trying to get them used to all kinds of terrain. We all survived, just barely.

At the end of June, I drove the thirty-five mile dirt road to Green River Lakes, ready for a trial overnight run into the wilderness. The first obstacle was the long wooden bridge over the lake's outlet. Carson was hesitant but got it together. While hiking around the lower lake, a group of Boy Scouts came up behind us with huge packs on their backs, towering over their heads. The llamas didn't recognize what these creatures were and took off. The two of us couldn't hang on to them although Marty tried and was dragged about fifteen feet over fallen logs and stumps. I yelled for him to let go and he finally did, a bit bruised and baffled.

Looked everywhere with the help of the boys and their leader. Suddenly Carson was spotted over a rise quite a distance away. I slowly approached and he actually waited and let me rope him. Daniel came willingly. Their panniers had come off; our sleeping bags and tent were scattered all over the place. After collecting our gear, Marty and I sat down in the grass to take stock of our situation and hesitantly decided to turn back. The bridge was easily accomplished but suddenly a mother moose appeared through the trees, her baby on the other side of the trail. Llamas are deathly afraid of moose. Carson bolted. Both of us grabbed Daniel's lead rope and wrapped it around a large tree trunk to hold him and watched, helpless, as Carson, with panniers bouncing wildly on either side, galloped up the trail and disappeared over a rise in a cloud of dust.

Daniel was secured, thanks to the tree, and finally, after he simmered down and stopped tugging at his rope, we carefully passed the moose family and continued up the trail to the parking lot where our truck and trailer were parked. Daniel was left in the trailer and the two of us started looking for Carson.

Some workmen clearing wood at the other side of the lot hadn't seen him. After combing the area he was finally found back in the parking lot. Daniel was half way out of the trailer, his belly hanging over the doors, stuck, trying desperately to get out. After getting them both back in safely, Marty and I looked at each other wondering what the hell we had gotten ourselves into. Mother Nature was throwing everything she could at us. Was she trying to tell us something?

Two weeks later, after having recuperated, Marty and I took the llamas with full packs for a two-hour walk to New Fork Lake just beyond our property. It went well.

Two days later, July 12th, our first overnight. Heading up the Pole Creek Trail from Elkhart Park, the 3.3 miles to Miller Park, a large open meadow filled with blue and mauve lupine was accomplished without mishap. A moderate descent via five switchbacks through a whitebark pine forest got us to Miller Lake, a peaceful sub-alpine large body of water in an open bowl with rocky bluffs to the north and forested slopes to the south. A pleasant site was found and the llamas were staked while the two of us unpacked, set up the tent and cooked dinner. The night passed uneventfully; the llamas were calm and we were relieved, to say the least. It was an easy walk out the next morning – nine miles, round trip.

Marty and I loved Carson and Daniel, our training was paying off, and I was in the Winds again.

The next week my oldest daughter, Karen, and her two daughters, Emily, eleven years old, and Kate, six years old, arrived from British Columbia. Marty and I had planned to take them into the Winds for three days and spent the next day packing. The food was the most fun. Sitting in our loft with legs dangling off the edge, they counted out the dried fruit, half going into the bags and half into their tummies. Because they had come from the coast and used to wearing t-shirts and shorts, and even though I had described in detail what to bring, they hadn't. So I dug out some old cashmere sweaters, wool hats and gloves, and bought them some long underwear on the way to the trailhead.

The first day was sunny with cloudy periods, at least until mid-afternoon. Then it started to rain and never stopped. A site was difficult to find because, not being able to make it up to Clear Lake, we were forced to camp at Big Sandy which was always very crowded. Our party consisted of five people, two tents and two llamas who needed space. There were hikers all over the place. It rained through the night and the next day and the next night and finally a decision was made to walk out.

On the way two hikers warned us of some sheepherders who had five aggressive dogs that ran at everybody on the trail. And we had llamas! Apprehensive, all of us watched at every bend in the path and suddenly there they were. Menacing marauders! Marty gave Karen the bear spray while we got off the trail with the llamas, giving them a wide birth. They came at her with teeth bared, barking. She held up the spray can, pressed the button and a sudden gust of wind turned the spray on her. "Help!" she cried, stumbling around with her arms stretched out in front of her. "I can't see anything." The two girls went crazy watching their helpless mother staggering off the path onto the uneven ground of the grassy meadow. I quickly handed the lead rope to Kate and told her to hang on for dear life. Marty gave his rope to Emily and off he and I went to rescue Karen. Walking her down to the stream and, wetting our neckerchiefs, her eyes and face were bathed with creek water. It took almost a half hour for her to get her sight back.

All there was to talk about after arriving home, very muddy and messy, was our wilderness adventure. They left after a few days, glad that we had spent the time together.

At the beginning of August, after weighing the llamas on a truck scale, 260 pounds each, (their weight determines what they can carry), our troupe left for an overnight at Upper Sweeney, a peaceful subalpine lake. The trail passed Miller Lake, descended to Middle Sweeney, and then to our destination, the prettiest of the three, surrounded by pine and spruce trees. All the sites were small and because room was needed for the boys, a spot too close to the trail was our only choice. In the morning a hike up a sloping meadow to an expansive grassy saddle that housed a large pond was easy. Some cowboys were trying to get their horses out of the water to move ahead. Staying well out of their way until they finally disappeared over the hill, the llamas behaved themselves. Continuing on to the junction of the Pole Creek Trail, the five miles out to Elkhart Park were relaxing. It was a satisfying walk without any mishaps.

A week later, August 7th, we did it again, this time parking our truck and trailer at Spring Creek Park and started the five miles to Glimpse Lake en route to Trapper Lake. After walking around the lily-covered pond, the trail climbed gently through an aspen forest, staying high above Fremont Lake, the largest in the range. Around the bend, the trees gave way to a narrow, open, very steep, sagebrush ridge, with the east side dropping precipitously to the lake far below. Marty and I freaked out. There was no turning back. The path was too narrow. The llamas were fine until Carson stopped in the middle of the mountainside to pee. The two of us stood there, panic-stricken, on a trail no more than a foot wide and five hundred feet long, with two 260-pound animals, our knees and hearts trembling. I waited for Carson. I had to because he wouldn't move until done what he was doing, and finally continued on until I reached a grove of trees. I looked back to see Marty close behind.

I remember now when I had called a woman who packed people on horses into the mountains and asked her about this trail, if there were any steep drop-offs and she said there weren't any, but then added, "Well, yes, I remember there's one that I don't like crossing when I'm on the back of a horse." I asked her how bad it was, and she replied, "If those kind of things bother you, you won't like it." This conversation took place a long time ago and I had forgotten. But I remembered it now. What was on both of our minds is that it would have to be done again on the way back.

Just beyond the Bridger Wilderness boundary, the blue waters of Glimpse Lake, at 4.8 miles, appeared through a forest of whitebark pine and fir. After descending one hundred and fifty feet into a rocky realm and crossing the lake's outlet, a climb to a ridge where the trail leveled out was achieved. After no more than a mile or so, Prospector Lake appeared, floating in a large grassy meadow. It looked very inviting and a decision was made to stop and make camp, still a bit shaken from the ridge we were just hanging off. The two of us were worn out – why push it!

The llamas were staked, the tent set up and my partner and I relaxed under a mid-afternoon sun. I sketched Daniel and Carson in the meadow surrounded by lupine, arnica and daisies, then waded in the water, apprehensive, not wanting to go on because of that bloody hillside. We were stuck.

Carson and Daniel at Prospector Lake

Day 2: Packed up in the morning and started out. Just before the precipice I told Marty not to look down, just look at the backs of my boots. As I crossed the midway mark without any mishaps, I shouted back, "only a few more feet to the trees." It was over before we knew it. When asked what was up ahead by some hikers, I warned them about the steep hillside. It didn't seem to bother them. A wonderful, uneventful walk out had us talking about our fears of which only the two of us understood.

Backpacking was different with animals. It was a lot more work, especially for two people not used to handling large animals. We had to think of others rather than ourselves. Are they comfortable? Well fed? Enough grass? Water? They came first. Going into the mountains was the one time I could concentrate on myself. I needed that in my life.

It took seventeen hours to get back to New Mexico. The llamas got out of the corral again. Our neighbor called to tell us they were playing on a dusty mound of earth at the edge of his property. They were retrieved quickly enough and easily brought home.

In the middle of May they were gelded, fighting teeth removed and toenails cut. It was quite an ordeal. Because the vet took his time about starting, the anesthetic had worn off and he couldn't grab their feet. Carson weighed two hundred eighty-five pounds and Daniel, two hundred ninety-five pounds.

222

On June 13th Marty and I left for Wyoming. At the beginning of July all of us walked four miles around Half Moon Lake just outside of Pinedale. Then, in the middle of the month, we packed up for an overnight and drove to the Trapper Lake Trailhead. After hiking a few miles the black flies forced us to turn back. The llamas sat down on the trail a few times and wouldn't move. They were so bothered by the flies on their bellies and in their eyes. It really was bad.

Our Daniel cabin had sold by then and building on our New Fork Lakes property next to the National Forest was being considered. Marty wasn't happy about the situation but I wanted to build. However, living in the tent, cooking outdoors, trying to construct a cabin and lugging around these two very large llamas was getting too difficult.

The two of us came to the decision that this plan just wasn't working. So the word was put out to see if there was anybody who wanted llamas. It didn't take long. Two couples, Sue and Rick with their two daughters, and Joann and Garry fell in love with our boys. Two of their eleven llamas were getting old. They drove from the Midwest every summer to their cabins south of Pinedale and trekked into the mountains, taking people along as well; they had been doing it for years and were thrilled.

A few days later Marty and I loaded Carson and Daniel into the trailer for the last time and dropped them off at their new home. We were sad driving away but relieved to go on with our lives. They had invited us to go into the Winds with them for a week and I was excited. Marty decided to pass on it and I went alone. This was the first time I would backpack with people I didn't know and had no idea what to expect.

XXIV

A New Experience in the Wilderness

August 2005:
At 5:00 a.m., I washed my hair, had some toast and tea with
Marty and left for Sue and Rick's house where he dropped me
and then returned home while I walked into the Winds for six
days. It was good seeing Carson and Daniel again.

Big Sandy Trailhead to Rapid Lake, eight miles, was our
destination – eleven people, eleven llamas, and two dogs – a
long line. Since I was the oldest of the bunch, I thought they
might be apprehensive about me being able to keep up. With
only a daypack on my back, I walked ahead with Sue, a school-
teacher, and Joann, a children's librarian. They had known one
another since they had met their husbands who were friends in
high school. Sue and Rick, with their daughters, Kristin and
Karen, had built their home just south of Pinedale a few years
ago, and now, Joann and Garry were constructing a cabin next to
them. Their dog, a Burmese Mountain Dog called Booner, was
along. Dave and Mary with their two sons, Beau and Nate, had
been invited because Nate and Kristin were high school buddies.
Dave was a police-pilot and Mary, a nurse. Their tiny, blind
dachshund sat atop Dave's pack. I was excited to be part of this
caravan and in the Winds again.

It was a peaceful walk until Big Sandy Lake when it started
to rain lightly along with some thunder and lightning. Stopped
for lunch at the south end of the lake, and because of the
lightning, Rick dispatched us in twos and threes to walk across
the open meadows around the lake.

There were four streams to ford barefoot and because Joann needed her water shoes that were packed with the llamas, already on the other side of the creek, she and I walked together, her leaning on me. She had arthritic feet and the rocks were difficult without shoes. Garry who had crossed leading the llamas, stood on the other side concerned. We made it, retrieved our sandals from the panniers, and had no further trouble.

One more mile up to Rapid Lake nestled in a picturesque valley with lots of room for the llamas. Roanne and I had been there four years ago in 2001, when she and I thought a bear ran by our tent. It began hailing upon our arrival. I set up my tent quickly under some trees but moved it when the sun came out. Mary and Dave set theirs near Sue and Rick's and their sons came over to help me but realized that I was doing fine by myself. Joann and Garry found a site away from all of us.

They all put up a large screened house, well away from the three tents, and started dinner – no bugs! – while the kids took care of the llamas, taking a few of them at a time down to the stream for water, then staking and feeding them in the meadow.

A dinner of tortillas, guacamole, enchilada sauce, beans and cheese was all fresh, packed in Colemans which hung from pulleys in the trees and cooked on three stoves while I had dried food – pasta, vegetables, pinto beans, two shitakes in a stew that I cooked on my tiny Whisperlite. They were well-equipped from having done this for years. Because they spent all their summers backpacking while their kids were growing up, they couldn't exist on dried fare for so long a time and carried about one hundred and fifty pounds of food in colemans, amazed at how little I had – a small sack for the whole trip. Roanne and I had learned to pack the minimum. It had taken us a few years to figure it out. They had also rigged a water purifying system from a tree branch and a continuous supply of wonderful cool, sparkling water was enjoyed by all. I didn't have to pump water on the entire trip. Such luxury!

After dinner, a walk up the valley in wet boots kept us in the sun until it disappeared. At dusk, back at our site, Nate kept us roaring with laughter while he acted out a theater piece from school – a very talented boy.

My tent was roomy, actually almost empty, with only me in it. It was strange without Roanne and I felt a little lost. Everything I had worn today was spread out to dry inside. All their gear was scattered over the rocks. The panniers had to be either covered in case of rain or everything inside of them needed to be in plastic. They did a bit of both.

A hawk screamed overhead. The llamas were in heaven in this high mountain pasture, and I thought about Marty and wished he were along. Rick and Garry mentioned him a lot and, maybe next year, they would get him up here. They talked about climbing East Temple. I didn't think I'd accompany them but maybe I'd get as high as I could. With Roanne along, I would have felt more secure.

It was a clear, still night. Clouds threatened in the west. The creek sounded in the distance. I was so happy to be here and felt comfortable to know there were a few inhabited tents nearby – especially without my daughter next to me. It was liberating and gave me a sense of being totally alone in the wilderness. I slept well – not needing the effort to listen.

Day 2: In the morning I did some yoga stretches. After breakfast all of us packed lunch and crossed the ridge from Rapid to Clear Lake in the adjacent valley. The girls and I went swimming in one of the frigid pools and then walked up to Deep Lake for lunch. Some of the guys went fishing at Temple Lake, while the rest of us just hung out, basking in the sun. These people were easy to be with. The afternoon hours crept by blissfully and when the sun was well past its zenith, a hike down to our tents was reluctantly initiated – just in time to start dinner.

Meals were a big deal with so many people to feed. I was astonished watching the preparations. I knew they were watching me as well with my one stove and one pot of stew. Lounging in the screened tent after dinner, all of us talked for hours. They wanted to hear about some of the hikes I had taken and told me about theirs. They had crossed Hay Pass down to the Golden Lakes which Roanne and I had never reached. Rick was shocked when he heard that the two of us walked alone and never took a gun into the mountains. He carried a revolver because he felt he had a lot of people to protect. It never had entered our minds.

A tough night. A mouse scurried under my tent and I couldn't scare it off. I was itchy around my elbows and thighs – small insect bites, I guessed, from having sat around the lake for so long. I thought a lot about Marty. I'm never really alone and this was a new experience for me. I read my book, wrote in my journal, and then lay there while my consciousness stretched to the edges of the valley, up and over the ridges into adjacent canyons, climbed the surrounding peaks and my topographic maps came alive, creating the landscape of which I was a part. A vast peaceful panorama – and I dozed on and off.

Day 3: Up at 8:00 a.m. During breakfast the clouds moved in. I took out my small bag of measured rolled oats, raisins and cinnamon and cooked it while those guys had fresh eggs, bacon, toast with jam and butter. Nate and Beau were intrigued by my meals and asked if they could try my food which surprised me and everybody in the tent. So few kids would actually ask. They loved it.

Joann, Rick and Dave decided to climb East Temple. The rest of us crossed the ridge once again to Clear Lake and over another to Black Joe Lake. I sketched the far side of this narrow valley while the girls shaved their legs down by the water; a hike up the lake to photograph some colorful columbines was refreshing while Garry fished at the far end. Everybody just did what they wanted. No group decisions. No feelings of having to join in. I returned to my drawing and relaxed while a cool breeze whispered through the trees and kept me comfortable; the waterfall across the lake unintentionally broke the silence.

Back over the ridges in time to prepare a large dinner of fresh cutthroat trout. I watched Joann and Sue as they removed all the bones that left the fish in tiny morsels. I wasn't used to this. When my father went fishing, he'd gut the fish and take out

Black Joe Lake

the bony spine in one shot. My pasta, lentils, vegetables, and mertensia leaves were delicious with a much-appreciated helping of fish.

After dinner I took a quick walk up the meadow with Garry and Joann to check the llamas, untangle Daniel, then hugged goodnight and disappeared into our respective tents. Daniel and Carson seemed to be doing well.

Day 4: I got up earlier than usual. A slight wind rustled the rainfly; clouds had moved in. It's been fun running around the mountains again. Tomorrow would be our last day. I was glad, I wanted to go home, but I'll miss this a lot. I forgot how I love to be here and am torn without Marty.

After breakfast all of us hiked down to Big Sandy Lake and crossed over to the trail that led to the Cirque of the Towers. Just above the first lake they all decided to climb Mitchell Peak. I didn't want to but they coaxed me into going as far as I could.

I got as far as I wanted and stopped along with Dave, who wasn't feeling well, and Mary, settling on a grassy ledge surrounded by boulders. Dave fell asleep and Mary and I talked about homeschooling. I had done it with Roanne for a year and she had with her sons for two years. Clouds moved in slowly. Suddenly it started to hail. A boulder sheltered us while putting on long pants. Lightning, thunder, rain and hail. Booner, who had stayed with us, didn't like it either.

The others were almost at the top. They had been climbing for about three hours when they abruptly turned around and started down because of the storm. It was dangerous being up so high, totally exposed, and the two of us worried about them. They couldn't move quickly because of the steepness. For some reason they got separated and finally Sue and Rick came down to us crouched against a huge boulder while the others took an alternate route, meeting us farther down the mountain. Garry was very upset that they didn't stick together. He lectured Kristin and Nate, who had taken off by themselves, having taught them never, under any circumstances, to get separated from the group. It was just too dangerous – everybody running around in the heights in different directions.

The sun finally came out. All of us got down safely to Big Sandy Lake and retrieved our sandals and water shoes that Garry had hidden under the bushes; crossed the four streams and headed up the trail to Rapid Lake. Mary didn't feel well so Joann and Dave stayed with her while the rest of us continued up through the woods and sent Beau, who was already at the site, down to help them. That evening Dave felt ill and remained in their tent while dinner was prepared, after which I went for a walk amongst the linden trees with Joann and Garry. Such incredible shapes – dead logs on the ground, twisted and gnarled, their limbs stretching out for somebody to acknowledge their presence.

The sky was slightly cloudy when I turned in and there was a light breeze – comforting.

Day 5: The next day was a major packing trip. Everything was taken down. All the panniers were packed, weighed and balanced. It took until noon to finally start out – an easy trip that took the rest of the day. I called Marty and it didn't take long for him to get there. All of us promised to do it again. I really had a good time, surprised as to how comfortable I had been. As long as I'm in the mountains I'm happy.

Upon our return to New Mexico, Marty became ill and had a gall bladder operation. Following our instincts as far as lightening our load had been wise and necessary. The trips into the mountains had become very difficult. We had been fortunate to find people who desperately wanted our llamas and lucky to sell our properties in Wyoming and have just one home. We needed a respite. I was sixty-five and Marty, seventy years old. It was time to slow down . . . a bit!

"The Mountains are calling and I must go."

John Muir - a letter to his sister in 1873

EPILOGUE

September 2006

Since the summer of 2002 when Roanne and I had hiked to North Fork Lake, Marty and I had moved back to Wyoming from Canada, then to Taos, New Mexico, and into three different houses there; the war in Iraq had started; Roanne and her partner had a baby boy and within a year decided to move to southern Oregon. Having lived on the high desert for so many years, she wanted something a little more lush. We couldn't imagine growing old without our grandson so Marty and I packed up and followed them West.

All this time I had kept Ken Koski's (the man we had met in 2002 who had ordered my book "Within the Earth a Mountain") letter in my desk drawer. I had never forgotten his sensitivity to the Wind Rivers and the promise I made to send him my next book about all my backpacking trips. It was eight years later, October 2010, when I emailed him about my newly published book. My message was returned. I googled him for his new address and what I got was a link to a website that made my heart stop.

September 11, 2006: "Search continues for man missing in Wind River Mountains." Ken Koski, Wyoming State Public Defender, missing from Pyramid Lake area.

I turned cold. I had to forcibly clear my mind to read on. His picture almost looked familiar but then I hadn't seen him clearly as we were all wrapped in hooded rain parkas on that high and very windy divide eight years ago.

Update: SEARCH DAY 2

Sublette County Search and Rescue personnel are continuing a search today for a backpacker who is believed to be missing in the Big Sandy area of the Wind River Mountains. The man, identified as 56-year-old Ken Koski, did not return from a backpacking trip last week.

According to a news release from the Office of the Wyoming State Public Defender's Office, Ken is a very experienced backpacker and is well familiar with the Wind River Range. He was camped alone near Pyramid Lake, last seen by an acquaintance on September 3rd on the trail to the lake, expected to return to Cheyenne by September 8th.

Koski was reported as a possible missing person on Saturday by backpackers in the area who were camped near him. They became concerned when they did not see any activity at his nearby tent site for several days. He was last known to be at his tent campsite on Tuesday, September 5th.

The Sublette County Sheriff's Office Search and Rescue teams went in on Sunday morning and have been joined by other crews from Teton and Fremont Counties. Helicopters have been provided by several agencies to conduct aerial reconnaissance of the remote and rugged terrain on both sides of the Continental Divide. Wyoming K-9 Search Dog teams are also working the area.

According to an update this morning on the website by the family, "Friends and family backpacked in and met the Sheriff's department at 9 a.m. at base camp. There is a group of horse searchers as well, but it takes a day on horseback to make the 12 miles in."

Update: SEARCH DAY 3

Press reports are indicating Ken Koski was supposed to return on Friday, September 8th; however his own entry in the hiker register log at the Big Sandy trailhead said he planned on coming out on Saturday, September 9th.

The Big Sandy area is popular with backpackers and technical rock climbers. Pyramid Lake is approximately 12 miles in from the Big Sandy Trailhead. It is very rugged terrain making search efforts extremely difficult. The high country received a dusting of snow on Friday night with more expected. Temperatures warmed and skies cleared Sunday and today.

Many people are working behind the scenes to help support the effort. Meals are being supplied by local stores and catering companies for 69-70 people.

Anyone who has seen Ken Koski since Wednesday, September 6th, or who has any information at all about his whereabouts, is asked to contact the Sublette County Sheriff's Office in Pinedale.

Big Sandy Lodge is very close to the search staging area, a location where people, vehicles and equipment are assembled before use. This is a remote location and this lodge does not have phone service, computer access or electricity. Emails sent to their website may not be checked for several days since the staff must come down off the mountain to check their email. Do not email Big Sandy Lodge for anything that is urgent or requires a quick response.

Update: SEARCH DAY 4

Organizers are now looking for volunteers to assist in the search. If you are interested in helping, contact the organizers with the following information: First & Last Name, Address, Phone Number, Physical Condition, Experience, Availability. E-mail this information and put "Volunteer" in the e-mail Subject Line. Please do NOT head out to help until you have been contacted by the team about how they can use your assistance. Additional dog teams arrived yesterday from Utah to help with the efforts.

DONATIONS
The Koski family asks that any donations go directly to the volunteer organizations that are conducting the search efforts. They do not want any money to come to the family.

234

Update: SEARCH DAY 5

"This is Day 5 of the intensive efforts which are being done on foot, horseback, with K-9 dogs and by helicopters . . . Many volunteers are also helping."

"Have hope! He is always prepared," wrote the Koski family who shared a number of their e-mails with us which talked about Ken. One point that came across very clearly is that the family has not given up hope. Ken is an experienced outdoorsman who carefully prepared for his trips into the backcountry. Even out on a day hike, Ken would be well dressed, carrying food, water and survival gear. Knowing this lends hope that even if he is injured somewhere, he may be hanging on waiting to be found. The Koski family's conviction and positive determination gives inspiration to everyone following this story and the search efforts

They sent this message saying: "We are very grateful for the tremendous effort and sincerely appreciate everyone's prayers and support."

Ken Koski's body found. September 14, 2006

The Sublette County Sheriff's Office has regrettably announced the finding of a body on the southeast side of Mount Bonneville, in Sublette County, today at about 11:50 a.m. by members of the Skinner Brothers Climbing Team out of Sublette County. Searchers will have to perform a tactical climb to get to the location of the body for further identification and recovery.

Update: 12:00 pm, Friday, September 15

Mr. Koski apparently fell approximately 400 to 500 feet from the summit of Mount Bonneville. It is not known why he fell. He landed in a crevice or on a ledge on the side of the mountain.

It is not believed that he was using a rope at all or even known if he was actually climbing. Officials believe he was on top of the mountain. The exact cause of death has not been officially announced, but with the distance he fell, the blunt trauma likely made the fall a fatal one.

The majority of the clothing Mr. Koski was wearing blended in with the terrain and rocks around him, making him very difficult to spot until the search climbers were very close to him. The terrain on the side of Mount Bonneville was a boulder field with many crevices. The area has a lot of crumbly "rotten rock," which could easily cause a fall.

The terrain ranges from 9,500 feet to 12,600 feet in elevation. Mount Bonneville is 12,585 feet, several miles northwest of Pyramid Lake. His last entry in his personal journal was on Tuesday, September 5th.

The two climbers who initially found him stayed with him on the side of the mountain until later in the afternoon after the weather cleared and the helicopters were able to fly safely back into the area. A long rope was attached and his body was lowered to the ground. He was then taken to a waiting helicopter and transported to the Pinedale airport, where his body was turned over to the Sublette County Coroner.

A helicopter later went back into the area and picked up the two rescuers who climbed back down to a safe area where the helicopter could land.

The Koski family wrote the following message posted on their website: "We simply cannot thank the search and rescue teams, friends, volunteers and the community enough. To everyone who came together to help us in the search or offer support by phone, email, and prayers, we Thank You."

They also said Ken loved Mount Bonneville because he said it was the one he always wanted to conquer. They quoted from a journal entry that he wrote: "There is no place that I would rather be than right here, right now, unless it was with my family."

The family wrote that as hard as this loss is on friends and family, if Ken were here, he would say, "That's life..." In a journal entry from a backpacking trip Ken and his son Chris took a month prior, Ken wrote, "Quitting is NEVER an option! Life is good."

How unbelievable! He was alive in my mind all these years and to find him dead was going to take some time getting used to. Had I known, I would have volunteered on that search.

My e-mail to Cheryl Koski
May 26, 2011

Dear Cheryl Koski,

I used to live in Wyoming and have hiked in the Winds for many years. On one such occasion in 2002 my daughter and I met Ken, his brother-in-law and some young boys with them. It was many years ago. We stopped to talk on one of the high passes and after realizing we had hiked to many of the same areas, I mentioned my book "Within the Earth a Mountain" that recounted our hikes in the Winds. Ken said he would like to buy an autographed copy and it was mailed to him upon my return.

After reading the book, he replied with a wonderful, very detailed letter discussing how he felt about some of my experiences in the wilderness and thanked me. He said he would also like to have a copy of my next book which was going to include my latest hikes into the Winds. I kept his letter, touched by his interest and sensitivity. That was August 2002.

It took another eight years for me to hear the news. I was not prepared for what I read and decided to write and express my sympathies to you and your family.

My next book that includes the hike on which we met Ken is almost finished. I read the entire website and couldn't get it off my mind. Would you kindly give me permission to include the account about Ken? Since he took the time to write that beautiful letter about reading my previous book and commented on so many of the paragraphs describing his thoughts on certain campsites and wildflowers in specific areas, I have never forgotten his empathy of the Wind Rivers, my favorite place to hike and obviously his.

Cheryl Koski's e-mail Response:
May 27, 2011

Dear Harriet,

I was very touched to receive this email from
you. I have learned so very much more about Ken
following his death and the people's lives he
touched. He was a remarkable man who loved life and
Wyoming.
Of course you can use his letter in your book. He
would be thrilled that you would consider to do
that. I would love to buy a copy of your book when
you get it published. If at all possible, I would be
thrilled if you could sign it. Ken has a complete
collection of books that are signed by authors so I
would add it. I will now look for your book that I'm
sure is in one of his bookshelves.
I looked at your website and your artwork is
beautiful! I am copying my children on this email so
they too can enjoy your work and note. You might be
interested to know they found Ken's daypack on top
of the mountain last September. The climber who
found it has anchored it in and hopes to go up this
summer to retrieve it for us.
How did you ever find me or get my email address?
I have only been at the VA for three years after I
retired from the State of Wyoming.
I look forward to hearing from you again and
reading your book.

Sincerely, Cheryl

My Response:

Hi Cheryl,

My dear friend Bonnie, who edited my last book, used to work in the Court system in Jackson Hole and knew a lot of public defenders. She heard of the accident and found you on the web. I will let you know of my book's progress.

Cheryl's Response:

```
    The internet has sure helped us all! I look
forward to hearing about your book.
```

The End

"We don't stop hiking because we grow old, we grow old because we stop hiking." Finis Mitchell

Please help - If you enjoyed my book, please post a review (even a few words) wherever you purchased the book or on Amazon. Reviews are the greatest way to help an author. And, please tell your friends. Reviews are a key part of the search algorithms that allow new readers to find my work.

https://www.amazon.com/Crossing-Boundary-Return-Wilderness-Freedom/dp/0933294107